HOME-BAKED BREAD

HOME-BAKED BREAD
Over 90 Recipes for Making Bread
Loaves, Rolls, and Baked Treats

First published September 2013
Copyright © 2013 by Hourglass Press LLC.

Hourglass Press LLC.
321 East Ninth Street
New York, NY 10003-7772
www.hourglasspress.com

Text © 2013 by Doris Goldgewicht
Photographs © 2013 by José Diaz, Carol Guzowski and Cuatro Fotografía
Editorial Direction: Susan Lauzau Editorial Services
Design © 2013 by Coral Communications Design LLC
www.coralcommunicationsdesign.com

This book is a single component of *HOME-BAKED BREAD* and is not intended to be sold separately.

First edition, Paperback, September 2013
ISBN: 978-1-935682-10-3
Library of Congress Cataloging-in-Publication data available upon request.
10 9 8 7 6 5 4 3 2 1
Printed in China

Please note: The publisher has made every effort to ensure the accuracy of the text, and every recipe in this book has been home-tested in an effort to assure that the information contained within is correct. Variations in consistencies will occur depending on altitude and experience; we encourage you to practice, practice, and enjoy!

CUATRO

Communications & Design

HOME-BAKED BREAD

Over 90 Recipes for Making Bread

Loaves, Rolls, and Baked Treats

DORIS GOLDGEWICHT

CONTENTS

THE BASICS

HEARTY YEAST-RISEN LOAVES

ROLLS & OTHER SAVORY YEAST BREADS

FAVORITE SWEET YEAST BREADS

MOUTHWATERING SAVORY QUICK BREADS

DELIGHTFULLY SWEET QUICK BREADS

HOLIDAY BREADS & SPECIAL TREATS

PREFACE

I firmly believe that every human being should have meaningful goals in life. This book has been one of my main aspirations, and into it I put all my effort, love, and dedication. Today, I am proud and pleased to present a work with more than 90 delicious recipes that have been tested and approved by the demanding palates of family, friends, students, staff, and professional cooks.

I truly hope you will enjoy this book, which is the product of years of work developing recipes. My decades of baking breads, rolls, quick breads, and other treats have taught me about the wonderful flavors and aromas that come about when you experiment with combining quality ingredients. Amazing forms and textures are possible when you mix and bake using different tools, ingredients, and techniques—the results have sometimes astonished me, and I hope you love them as well!

—Doris Goldgewicht
doris@tipscr.com

ACKNOWLEDGMENTS

I owe my culinary education to many people:

First, my husband, Israel, because he tested everything to make sure that what comes out of my kitchen is delicious. What love! I really miss you....

My children, both my son and daughter and their families, who always gave me healthy criticism that encouraged me to grow.

Hans, my dad, who throughout his life taught me to differentiate tastes and smells, to investigate and experiment with textures, and to try new things without fear... What beautiful memories!

My mom, Anita, and my in-laws, Rosita and Enrique, as well as the rest of my family and my friends. I love the enthusiasm with which they have greeted all my experiments.

My nana, Ata, a lovely old lady, to whom I owe my love of cooking. She always allowed me to get dirty and make a big mess in her kitchen. I lost her two years ago.

My grandmother, Rosa—I owe to her the smells of my childhood, the neatness of a white apron, the pleasures of a spice cupboard smelling of cinnamon, chocolate, and vanilla.

There are also those other friends, chefs, who have entrusted me with their culinary secrets.

I also want to include teachers, those wonderful beings who have made me a lover of the culinary arts, who taught me to transform, to investigate, to experiment without fear....

Sometimes we find soul mates who are with us through thick and thin. I have the privilege of sharing special moments with Elita, my sister, and Elena, my true friend, who collaborated with love in the realization of this dream.

Special thanks to my photographers and friends Jose Diaz and Veronica Quiros, for their commitment to the pictures. Each of the dishes presented here will inspire you to try the recipes.

Marcela Carranza E. and Tobel Cosiol, thank you very much for your time to kitchen-test these recipes and prepare them for the photography shots, you are wonderful bakers.

Special thanks to my amazing friends, Carol Guzowski and Evelyn Birbragher, who encouraged me to do this book.

My thanks go to Hourglass Press for introducing to my baking techniques and recipes to North America, and to Carol Guzowski for creating an elegant and modern design for this book.

And I left dessert for last... my beloved grandchildren, with whom I share all my wisdom and to whom I dedicate this book, because it represents, after all, a message of love for them.

INTRODUCTION

Nothing is more delicious than home-baked bread, warm from the oven—don't you agree? And it's easier than you think for a home baker to turn out nutritious, fresh, flavorful breads, rolls, and quick breads with a minimal investment of time, equipment, and practice. If you follow my simple step-by-step instructions, measuring your ingredients carefully and taking no shortcuts with the recipe, I assure you that your next loaf will surpass most of the breads you can find on the shelves of your local supermarket. With a little practice, your breads will rival those of your town's best bakery!

After all, if our grandmothers could turn out loaf after delightful loaf of homemade bread using primarily their hands and locally available ingredients, imagine what we can produce given our modern appliances and all of the wonderful specialty ingredients available to us today on grocery shelves and via the internet. The conveniences of modern life are intended to cut back on the amount of work and increase the fun, and we should take full advantage of this, even as we embrace the age-old tradition of producing healthy, hearty baked goods for our families.

I invite you into a world of joyful experimentation. In *Home-Baked Breads*, you'll find scores of easy-to-follow recipes that lead you through the steps that will put rustic loaves, dinner rolls, savory holiday breads, sweet treats, and other delicious goodies on your table. Join me in the kitchen, and you will quickly learn why it is said that baking is an art. Put aside your thoughts of the kitchen as a place of monotonous daily chores, and free yourself to experiment with the range of fresh and tasty breads featured in this book.

And when you offer your wonderfully flavorful breads to your friends and family and ask, "Do you like it?" you will be able to say with amazing pride, "I made it!"

THE BASICS

Baking is a science as well as an art, and there are many books that detail the complexities of forming gluten, the inner lives of yeast, and the physics of the baking process. These books are truly fascinating, and well worth checking out if you want to understand the intricate scientific principles involved in producing bread.

This book is not going to repeat that material, however: like many home bakers, I am interested primarily in making a variety of breads and baked goods that are tasty and can be made easily in the average kitchen. It's important, though, to know why certain ingredients and methods are critical, so what follows is a short course in the things you really need to know and consider when you're baking at home.

Ingredients

Choosing top-quality ingredients does not guarantee that your baked goods will be delectable, but it certainly contributes to a superior result. Quality ingredients are the construction materials that help build a good bread. The flour, starches, eggs, water or other liquids, sugar, fats, baking powder, baking soda, yeast, and salt must all be fresh and of good quality to yield a rich and flavorful bread.

The proteins found in the flour, starch, and eggs give mass, body, and structure to the things we bake. Fats—butter, lard, oil, or other fats—provide softness and texture, and in some cases, flavor. These ingredients lubricate the proteins and soften them. The type of fat used can alter the texture of the finished product. Vegetable oil, for example, gives a softer product than butter because oil is liquid and butter is solid.

Other softeners include sugar: when sugar comes into contact with water and leavening agents such as baking soda or yeast, the pH balance (acidity or alkalinity) of the mixture changes. The size of the air cells formed in the batter or dough is also affected by the pH.

Not surprisingly, water and other liquid ingredients provide moisture to dough. Eggs and syrups moisturize dough as well. In fact, eggs serve many purposes, from moisturizing (via their liquid) to providing structure (because of their protein content), which is why they are often called the stars of baking.

Salt, flavorings, liqueurs, and spices all lend special flavor to baked goods, but they are somewhat less critical to the success of the outcome. You'll still want to measure them carefully because flavor balance is important, but being a little bit off in your measurement with a flavoring is less likely to cause outright failure of your bread-baking attempt than mismeasuring other types of ingredients.

Most of the recipes in this book can be made using ingredients found on the shelves of your local supermarket, though there are some items that will be more readily available in some neighborhoods than in others. For that reason, we've included in the appendix a list of internet resources that carry specialty baking items.

FLOUR

The type of flour you use plays a crucial role in the development of a good bread. Bread flour, available in some stores and online, has a higher protein content, typically between 11 and 13 percent. This leads to better rising for yeast breads and yields a dough that stands up well to mechanical kneading. In fact, to develop the gluten fully and get a richer bread, you must beat or knead dough made with bread flour a little more than dough made with all-purpose flour (photo 1). It's worth getting bread flour, if you can, for many recipes, especially those with a more rustic feel (some of the recipes here specifically suggest it), though for smaller rolls, bread flour can make a crust that is a bit too chewy given the small surface area. For these baked goods, you may wish to use either a mixture of bread flour and all-purpose flour or all-purpose flour alone.

In fact, most of us home bakers are happy to make our bread only with all-purpose flour—it has less protein than bread flour (all-purpose flour's protein content is typically between 8 and 10 percent), and thus yields a softer result. Note that some suppliers sell all-purpose flours with a protein content higher than this—if you're buying from a specialty retailer, check the content on the label.

Some of the recipes in this book call for other types of flour, specifically whole wheat flour (photo 2), or cassava flour (photo 3), usually to be mixed with all-purpose flour. Whole wheat flour is white flour before the bran and the germ have been milled out. Bread made with whole wheat flour has a nuttier flavor and a denser texture than that made with white flour only. Cassava flour, made from the cassava plant and a common ingredient in many South American breads, is also known as tapioca flour (tapioca starch is somewhat different, as it isolates the starch from the cassava).

Be sure to store your flour in an airtight container. You can transfer the flour to a tightly lidded container, or you may leave it in its original packaging and put it inside a sealable plastic bag. Squeeze as much air from the bag as you can before sealing it closed. Properly stored, white flour has a shelf life of about one year, while whole wheat flour's shelf life is only about three months. If you don't plan to use your whole wheat or cassava flour within three months, store it in your freezer in a tightly sealed plastic bag.

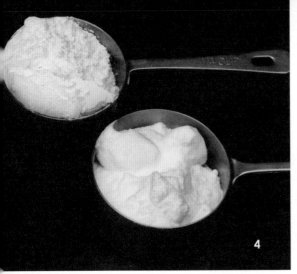

BAKING POWDER & BAKING SODA

These leavening agents help baked goods rise because they form carbon dioxide when they come into contact with liquid and heat. Though both baking soda and baking powder (photo 4), will keep for a long time on pantry shelves, it's very important that these ingredients are still potent when you use them—if they're not, your baked goods will turn out flat and heavy.

If you're in any doubt about their effectiveness, you can test them easily. For baking powder, just drop ¼ teaspoon into ½ cup of hot tap water; the baking powder should begin to effervesce immediately. Testing baking soda requires the addition of an acid: stir ¼ teaspoon of vinegar into the ½ cup hot water before adding ¼ teaspoon baking soda. If the baking powder or baking soda does not bubble on contact with the liquid, or if the reaction seems lazy, make a visit to the store for a fresh container.

SUGAR

Sugar is so important in making baked goods—it gives sweetness, color, and softness to your creations. Too much sugar, though, can affect the ability of the dough to rise. As with all ingredients in baking, it's important to measure carefully. Recipes with larger amounts of sugar typically have larger amounts of yeast to compensate. Of course, quick breads, which use baking powder as leavening, are not affected. Brown sugar (photo 5), can be substituted for white sugar (photo 7), use ⅔ of the quantity of white. Powdered sugar (also called confectioner's sugar, photo 6), is used to sprinkle and for glazing.

Sifting sugar is important, as it helps support the air cells in the bread and breaks up any clumps that may be caused by moisture in the air. Store sugar in a tightly sealed container and it will keep indefinitely.

YEAST

A single-celled organism, yeast feeds on sugars, producing carbon dioxide that makes your dough rise. It also produces alcohol, which further expands the dough when it heats up in the oven. This is why your dough will rise a bit more once it begins baking. (The alcohol cooks off during baking, so don't worry about producing alcohol-laced breads!) There are basically three types of yeast widely available to the home baker. Most of the recipes in this book call for instant yeast, as it is the most forgiving and easiest to find, but for those who prefer other types, I have provided a yeast equivalency table in the appendix. Please note all yeasts look very similar, but they perform differently.

Fresh Yeast

Fresh yeast (photo 1), may be found in the refrigerator section of your grocery, though fewer and fewer stores are carrying it these days. Fresh yeast (sometimes called baker's yeast) must be kept refrigerated—it must not be stored at temperatures above 42°F because higher temperatures damage the yeast cells and the yeast may become ineffective. The advantage of fresh yeast is the wonderful flavor it gives the breads—there is nothing quite like it! Be careful, however, not to use fresh yeast after the expiration date on the package. Also, it will dry out and lose its leavening properties after a few days once the package is opened, so discard any leftover yeast that you don't plan to use right away.

Active Dry Yeast

Active dry yeast (photo 2), must be activated in warm water with sugar or honey. It gives excellent elasticity, aroma, and flavor to your breads. Dry yeast should be added at the start of mixing. Its shelf life is about twelve months if it is stored in an airtight container in a cool, dry place or in the refrigerator.

Instant Yeast

This type (photo 3), of yeast is air-dried and sold vacuum packed. It is highly practical because its shelf life is two years when it is stored optimally, though after the package is opened the yeast will gradually lose its effectiveness. This type of yeast can be mixed directly into the flour or other dough ingredients without being hydrated first, like active dry yeast. Store it in an airtight container in the refrigerator or in a cool, dry place. For years, I worked mainly with instant yeast and it gave me such great results that I almost forgot about the other types!

1 2 3

FATS

Some breads—ciabatta, for example—contain no fats, while others—such as brioche—are rich with flavorful butter. Many of the recipes in this book call for vegetable oil (photo 4), or butter (photo 6), though olive oil (photo 5), and shortening are also specified for certain breads. If a recipe calls for butter, always use unsalted, so as not to throw off the salt balance in the dough.

Store your butter tightly wrapped in the refrigerator for up to three months. It will keep in the freezer for about a year. Olive oil, vegetable oil, and other oils you may choose to substitute will oxidize over time, giving them a rancid flavor. Store your oils tightly capped in a cool, dark cabinet, as light and heat will hasten their demise. Typical shelf life for an opened bottle of oil, stored optimally, is one year.

SALT

Salt is a crucial ingredient in enhancing the flavor of bread, though typically very little is used. Without it, though, your bread would taste flat and bland. It also plays a role in strengthening the dough's gluten structure and slowing the pace of yeast activity, both important chemical developments in bread baking. These recipes were developed using table salt (photo 7). Kosher or sea salt (photo 8), may be substituted, but note that these salts are coarser grained. Because of the variability of grain size by type of salt and even by brand (Morton's Kosher and Diamond Crystal Kosher salt are quite different, for example), a precise substitution is difficult to make, but you will need 50 percent to 70 percent more than if you use table salt. Because salt can kill yeast, it is best to add it to the opposite side of the bowl from the spot where you are adding the yeast, or mix the yeast with other ingredients thoroughly before adding the salt.

Measuring Ingredients

Measuring ingredients is of vital importance in baking. Professional bakers weigh rather than measure their ingredients, and the exact formulas they use give a consistent and reliable product; adding ingredients by weight also helps control costs. For home baking, this method is not entirely practical. In this book, I will work with measurements, because this is easiest and most affordable for you. When I measure dry ingredients, I use dry measure cups and spoons and measure flush with the top of the cup.

Liquid ingredients should be measured using a measuring cup for liquids. But, of course, at the same time that measuring ingredients is important in baking, the amount of liquid a recipe requires will vary with the humidity of the environment, the precise type of flour used, and the moisture level in the flour and other dry ingredients. For this reason, some of the recipes direct you to add water (or milk), then add more as required until the dough reaches the consistency described. A little practice will make you more confident in knowing when you've added the proper amount. Typically, once all the loose flour in the bowl is incorporated and you have a workable, though somewhat sticky, dough, you have reached the right amount of liquid.

Note: Some of the recipes call for increments of half a tablespoon, a measure that is included in many measuring spoon sets but not all. If you don't happen to have a ½ tablespoon measure: ½ tablespoon = 1½ teaspoons.

Please see page 20 for illustrations of these measuring tools.

Making the Starter Dough (Sponge)

Some bread doughs are made in two stages (and some sourdoughs in three), beginning with a starter dough, also called sponge or yeast starter. Starter dough typically consists of part of the total dough's flour, all or part of the water, and all or part of the yeast (photos 1 and 2), which are mixed together and allowed to ferment for a period of time (photo 3). Once the starter dough has fermented for the recommended period of time, it is mixed with the remaining dough ingredients and kneaded to develop the gluten.

1   2   3

Because of the additional fermenting time allowed the yeast, breads made with this two-step process are fuller in flavor. It also improves the texture of the bread, because the extended fermentation helps activate enzymes that leaven the bread.

Breads made in this way are no more difficult than "straight doughs," those made without pre-ferment, but they do take a bit longer because of the time needed to rest the starter dough.

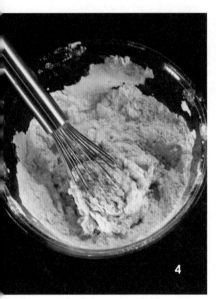

Making the Dough

Mixing distributes all the ingredients evenly—making sure that yeast and salt are well mixed helps the bread rise (photo 4). For straight doughs, the addition of liquid to the yeast also starts the fermentation process.

After mixing, the dough is kneaded—worked either by hand (photo 5) or by machine. This brings oxygen into the dough and develops the gluten, giving yeast breads their characteristic texture. For most yeast doughs, the more they are kneaded the better the bread will be. Dough should be springy and elastic (photo 6). There are exceptions, however, where the dough should be minimally worked, and these are noted in individual recipes. (Quick breads and some other baked goods do not require kneading—and in fact, should not be worked too much—as they are leavened by agents other than yeast.) The kneading times in recipes, unless otherwise noted, is for kneading with a stand mixer—if you are hand kneading, you will need to add five to ten minutes or even more (depending on how vigorously you knead) to the time.

 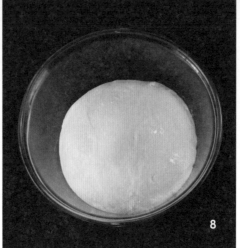 

To work dough by hand, spread flour lightly over a flat surface (photo 7). Put the dough on the surface, push the palms of your hands into the dough, spreading it out; then fold the dough over, rotate it, and push down again, this is called kneading. Continue until the dough is smooth and elastic. As you work with dough, you will doubtless find your own method and rhythm. You can also knead by machine, and this will save time and effort on your part. A heavy-duty stand mixer fitted with a dough hook is best for kneading most bread dough—anything lighter is bound to burn out when heavy kneading is required. Make sure the dough is well mixed before beginning to knead by machine, or it may stick to the dough hook and simply spin around. Very sticky doughs are more easily kneaded using a stand mixer. Follow the instructions for your model to get additional advice on settings and kneading times.

The dough will then need to rest (photo 8), so that the yeast can rise. Individual recipes recommend how much the dough should rise (for example, to twice its original size) and/or how long it should rest (for example, two to three hours). Once the dough has risen (photo 9) for the recommended period and it is time to "punch down" the dough, slide your hands under the dough, lift it up, and fold it over, so that pockets of built-up gas are released but the gluten structure is not harmed. Some bakers like to "punch down" the dough more vigorously; be careful not to handle the dough excessively, though, as this can damage the gluten.

Once the dough is ready, it is formed into its final shape, whether loaf, roll, ring, or other form. Recipes throughout guide you in how the bread should be shaped. Some dough must be pressed with the fingers or rolled with a rolling pin on a floured surface into a desired thickness and shape. Others are simply cut and shaped into balls or other forms.

Baking

Ovens are highly individual, and even ovens of the same brand and model may vary. The more familiar you are with your oven and its eccentricities, the better baker you will be. Does it have hot spots? Does it bake more in the rear than in the front? Does the temperature drop dramatically when you open the door, or does the heat hold fairly steady? Buying an oven thermometer will be helpful, as the factory-set temperatures are not always accurate, particularly if the oven is an older model. Get to know your oven's tricks.

The oven should be preheated to the temperature indicated in the recipe, and bread dough placed into the hot oven. When baking, place the rack in the middle or lower third of the oven. The heat should come from below. When making bread, do not turn on the top heating element, if this is an option on your oven, as your bread will quickly form a crust that can be deceptive. A well-baked crust may trick you into believing that the bread is ready when the dough is still raw in the center.

Some of these recipes call for breads to be baked with steam, which promotes maximum oven spring and a good crust. Professional bread baking ovens have steam injectors, but home bakers need to be a bit more creative. I advocate in this book the safest method of adding steam to the baking process, but be aware that steam is not good for all ovens, particularly models with digital controls. Evaluate your own situation and decide whether you will risk damaging your oven if you introduce steam.

If you decide to bake with steam, place a cast-iron pan on the lowest rack of the oven when you preheat it. Immediately after placing bread in the oven, carefully drop several ice cubes into the pan. The cubes will melt and produce steam at the beginning of the baking process, then the oven will dry out, which is what you want.

Watch the bread as it nears the end of its baking time. Most breads will turn a rich golden color—the precise timing may vary by five minutes or so.

After removing the bread from the oven, place it on a wire cooling rack. Individual recipes advise when to remove bread baked in pans.

Pans

Buy bread pans and baking sheets of good, strong materials. Grease them well and flour them or, better still, use parchment paper at the bottom of the pans. Here's a tip: when you buy a new pan, wash it very well and then dry it. Rub it with a thin layer of vegetable or olive oil and bake it for thirty minutes at 350 degrees. This will season the pan and greatly reduce the chance of baked goods sticking. Don't wash the pans after use, just wipe them well with a paper towel or clean cloth.

The pans most commonly needed in this book include baking sheets, 13-by-9-inch pans, 8- or 9-inch round pans, and standard loaf pans measuring approximately 5 by 9 inches. There are, however, recipes that call for specialty pans as well, ranging from Christmas tree–shaped pans to brioche pans. Where possible, I suggest alternatives to the specialty pans recommended.

1. Pullman loaf pan
2. Baking sheet
3. Mini loaf pan
4. Ring-shaped pan

Other Equipment

Following is the core team of kitchen tools that will serve you well for making the recipes in this book.

1. Heavy-duty stand mixer
2. Mixing bowls in graduated sizes
3. Strainer
4. Whisk
5. Rubber spatula
6. Sifter
7. Sharp knife
8. Rolling pin
9. Pastry brush*
10. Oven thermometer
11. Wooden spoons
12. Parchment paper
13. Vegetable peeler
14. Zester
15. Oven mitts
16. Wire cooling racks
17. Tongs
18. Scissors
19. Measuring spoons
20. Dry measuring cups
21. Liquid measuring cup
22. Baking pans*
23. Napkin*
24. Bamboo board*

*Included in Kit

Happy Baking!

With a bit of patience and practice, and a minimum of ingredients and equipment, you, too, can produce delicious, healthy breads and rolls at home. The more you bake bread, the more you will wonder—why haven't I done this before?" Be happy, bake bread at home, and tell me about your efforts: doris@tipscr.com.

Pura vida from Costa Rica!

HEARTY YEAST-RISEN LOAVES

Mini Loaves with Herbes de Provence • French Bread • French Bread with Herbs • Ciabatta • Potato Bread • Buttermilk–Oat Bread • Sourdough Bread • Garlic and Parsley Bread • Pesto-Filled Bread • Bread Stuffed with Roasted Peppers, Walnuts, and Basil • Rustic Bread with Dill and Oregano • Challah • Brown Bread with Poppy and Caraway • Fresh Herb Bread • Peppery Cheese Bread • Five-Grain Bread • Basil Spiral Bread • Basil-and-Cheese-Filled Bread • Focaccia Stuffed with Olives • Garlic and Rosemary Focaccia • Focaccia with Roasted Tomato and Basil Sauce • Pizza Bread • Olive Bread

MINI LOAVES WITH HERBES DE PROVENCE

Flavored with the herbs of southern France, these miniature loaves are a charming addition to any luncheon or special supper.

Ingredients

3½–4 cups flour
1 tablespoon instant yeast
2 eggs
1½ cups buttermilk
3 tablespoons unsalted butter, melted
2 tablespoons olive oil
½ teaspoon each: black pepper, oregano, garlic powder, herbes de Provence
1 teaspoon salt
   olive oil, for brushing

Preparation

1. Mix all ingredients well. The dough will be very soft.
2. Cover with plastic wrap and let double in size, 2 to 3 hours.
3. Grease eight mini loaf pans. Spoon dough into greased mini loaf pans. Let dough rise 20 minutes.
4. While dough is rising, preheat oven to 350°F.
5. Brush tops of dough with oil and bake until golden, 20 to 25 minutes. Cool on wire rack.

Difficulty

Easy

Preparation

3 hours

Portion

8 mini loaves

FRENCH BREAD

The hardest thing about this recipe is to stop eating! A crusty exterior and a soft crumb make this loaf a hearty treat. If you want to increase the fiber, swap out 1½ cups of the white flour with whole wheat flour.

Preparation

1. Mix the flour with the salt and sugar. Stir well and add the yeast.
2. Add the shortening and 1 cup of water to form a sticky dough. If dough is too dry, slowly add more water until all flour is incorporated and dough is sticky. Beat about 5 minutes. Place in greased plastic bag and let double in size, at least 3 hours.
3. Punch down dough and knead, adding flour until the dough is smooth and elastic. Divide into two pieces.
4. Form two long loaves. With a sharp knife, make cuts along the top of each loaf, and place on baking sheets lined with parchment paper sprinkled lightly with flour.
5. Let stand, covered, for 30 minutes. Using a pastry brush, brush the loaves with warm water. If desired, sprinkle poppy seeds on top.
6. Preheat oven to 400°F. Place a cast-iron skillet on a lower shelf of your oven, beneath the shelf you will use to bake the bread.
7. Sift flour lightly over each loaf.
8. When you put the bread into the oven, drop ice cubes into the cast-iron skillet to create steam.* Bake until golden, about 25 minutes.
   *Note that steam can be damaging to some ovens, particularly the newer digitally controlled ovens.

Ingredients

5 cups flour, plus extra
1 tablespoon salt
1 teaspoon sugar
1½ tablespoons instant yeast
3 tablespoons melted shortening
1 cup warm water, plus more as needed
1 tablespoon poppy seeds, for sprinkling (optional)

Difficulty

Easy to Intermediate

Preparation

3 to 4 hours

Portion

2 loaves

FRENCH BREAD WITH HERBS

Crusty and chewy, this French bread is seasoned with fresh herbs for extra pizzazz.

Ingredients

4½	cups flour, plus extra
1	tablespoon salt
1	tablespoon sugar
1½	tablespoons instant yeast
⅓	cup melted butter
3	tablespoons fresh herbs, such as basil, oregano, and rosemary, finely chopped
1	cup warm water, plus more as needed
	water, for brushing loaves

Preparation

1. Mix 3½ cups of the flour with salt and sugar. Add the yeast and stir.
2. In a separate bowl, mix melted butter with the herbs and 1 cup warm water. Add the water–butter–herb mixture to the flour mixture.
3. Add enough water to form a sticky dough and mix about 10 minutes in a stand mixer or 15 minutes by hand.
4. Place in a greased plastic bag and let double in size, at least 3 hours.
5. Punch down dough and knead. Add remaining flour, a little at a time as needed, until the dough is smooth and elastic.
6. Form three or four long loaves and place on baking sheets lined with parchment paper and sprinkled with flour.
7. With a sharp knife, make several cuts across the tops of the loaves.
8. Preheat oven to 400°F. Place a cast-iron skillet on oven rack below the rack on which you'll be baking the bread.
9. Cover loaves and let stand 30 minutes. Brush loaves with water and sprinkle with sifted flour.
10. When you put the bread into the oven, drop several ice cubes into the cast-iron skillet to create steam.* Bake until golden, 20 to 25 minutes.

    *Note that steam can be damaging to some ovens, particularly newer digitally controlled models.

Difficulty

Easy to Intermediate

Preparation

5 hours

Portion

3 loaves

CIABATTA

A rustic Italian yeast bread with a crisp crust and chewy interior, ciabatta is wonderful for hearty sandwiches or for dipping into fruity olive oil.

Ingredients

For the dough starter (sponge):
1   cup bread flour, plus extra
½   teaspoon sugar
½   teaspoon instant yeast
⅔   cup warm mineral water
For the dough:
3   cups bread flour, plus extra
½   teaspoon instant yeast
1   teaspoon salt
1   tablespoon powdered milk (can be skim)
1¼ cups warm mineral water

Preparation

1. Make the dough starter (sponge): The night before making the bread, mix all starter ingredients together. Cover and leave at room temperature overnight.
2. Make the dough: Mix flour, yeast, salt, and powdered milk in the bowl of a stand mixer. Add the dough starter and mix.
3. Add the mineral water and mix about 6 minutes. Dough will be very sticky. Cover and let dough rise until doubled in size, about 3 to 4 hours.
4. Preheat oven to 425°F.
5. Flour the table and your hands. Divide the dough into two rectangles about 8 by 20 inches each. Sift a little flour over the loaves. Cover with plastic wrap and let rise about 30 minutes.
6. Stretch rectangles out a bit, and place on baking sheets lined with parchment paper. Wet your hands and use them to wet tops of breads. Sift flour over the bread again.
7. Bake 20 to 25 minutes.

Difficulty

Easy to Intermediate

Preparation

4 hours and 1 day

Portion

2 loaves

POTATO BREAD

Potatoes, buttermilk, and flour come together to create a homey flavor and a dense yet moist consistency.

 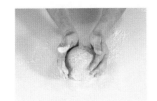 

Preparation

1. Peel the potatoes. Cut into chunks and boil in water until they are very soft, about 20 to 25 minutes.
2. Blend the potatoes with 1¾ cups water in a blender or with a hand blender until mixture resembles a thin puree.
3. In a separate bowl, mix the white flour and the whole wheat flour with the salt and sugar. Stir in the yeast. Set aside.
4. Combine the potato puree with vegetable oil, parsley, cheese, buttermilk, and eggs.
5. Form a well in the flour mixture and stir potato mixture into the center of the flour. Combine until a sticky but manageable dough forms. Stir with a wooden spoon (or mix in a stand mixer) about 2 minutes. Place the dough in a greased bowl, cover it tightly, and let it rise 3 hours.
6. Punch down dough to release the gas and knead a few minutes, adding flour if necessary to make the dough sticky yet workable.
7. Form dough into two balls. Grease and flour a baking sheet. Place the dough on the baking sheet at least 2 inches apart.
8. Mix 2 tablespoons water with the cornstarch.
9. Preheat oven to 400°F. Place cast-iron skillet on oven rack below the rack on which you'll be baking the bread.
10. Brush the dough with half the cornstarch mixture and then cut an "X" into the top of each ball. Let rise 20 minutes. Brush again with the cornstarch mixture.
11. When you put the bread into the oven, drop several ice cubes into the cast-iron skillet to create steam.* Bake until brown, approximately 30 minutes.
    *Note that steam can be damaging to some ovens, particularly the newer digitally controlled ovens.

Ingredients

2	medium potatoes
1¾	cups water
2	cups white flour
2	cups whole wheat flour
2½	teaspoons salt
3	tablespoons sugar
2	teaspoons instant yeast
3	tablespoons vegetable oil
2	tablespoons finely chopped fresh parsley (or 1 tablespoon dried)
½	cup crumbled semi-hard cheese, such as Colby, baby Swiss, or mozzarella
1	cup buttermilk
2	eggs
2	tablespoons water
2	tablespoons cornstarch

Difficulty

Easy to Intermediate

Preparation

5 hours

Portion

2 loaves

BUTTERMILK–OAT BREAD

That taste! This is similar to the bread served at one of my favorite restaurants ... and I tell the owner I visit his restaurant mostly for the bread!

Preparation

1. Mix water, 1 tablespoon honey, and yeast. Stir and let sit about 6 minutes.
2. Combine the flour and salt with the oats and mix well. Add the yeast mixture, buttermilk, the remaining honey, molasses, oil, and the 2 eggs. Add more warm water if needed to form a sticky dough.
3. Beat about 5 or 6 minutes. Place in greased bowl, cover, and let rise until doubled in size, about 3 to 4 hours.
4. Mix the walnuts into the dough.
5. Cut the dough into three equal parts. Stretch each piece into a rectangle about 14 by 10 inches and roll it tightly to form a small loaf (see photo). Place loaves about 1 inch apart on baking sheet lined with parchment paper.
6. Cover dough in plastic wrap and let rise an additional 15 minutes. While dough is rising, preheat oven to 400°F.
7. With a sharp knife, make across tops of loaves. Brush loaves with egg white and sprinkle with oats. Bake until the bread is golden brown and loaves sound hollow when tapped on the bottom, approximately 20 to 25 minutes. Cool on wire rack.

Ingredients

½	cup warm water
½	cup honey
1½	tablespoons dry yeast granules
2⅓	cups flour, plus extra
1	tablespoon salt
1¼	cups oats, plus extra for sprinkling
1½	cups buttermilk
2	tablespoons molasses
¼	cup vegetable oil
2	eggs
1	cup walnuts, finely chopped
1	egg white, beaten

Difficulty

Easy to Intermediate

Preparation

5 hours

Portion

3 loaves

SOURDOUGH BREAD

Because sourdough bread relies in part on naturally occurring yeasts that take time to ferment, it requires a larger outlay of time (though not necessarily of effort, as much of it is resting time). This crusty bread has the classic, slightly tangy taste that comes from the lactic acid produced during fermentation.

Preparation

1. Make part 1 of the starter: combine the 1 cup of the water and ½ teaspoon yeast until dissolved. Stir in the rest of the ingredients from part 1 of starter (buttermilk, plain yogurt, flour, semolina, and grapes) and let stand at room temperature 12 hours. Before using, remove the grapes and squeeze the juice through the cloth. Discard the grapes.
2. Make part 2 of the starter: combine the ½ teaspoon yeast with the 2 cups water and stir well with semolina, flour, and mixture from step 1. Let ferment for 4 hours.
3. Make the dough: combine the ¾ teaspoon yeast and ¾ cup water. Add the white flour, whole wheat flour, starter mixture, and salt.
4. Mix about 6 minutes. Refrigerate 12 hours.
5. Remove from refrigerator and let stand 4 hours at room temperature.
6. Preheat oven to 400°F. Place cast-iron skillet on oven rack below the rack on which you'll be baking the bread.
7. Form 2 round loaves, and place them on baking sheets that have been greased and floured or lined with parchment paper. Alternatively, you could use greased and floured round pans. Let dough double in size, 3 to 5 hours.
8. Make cuts on the tops of the loaves. Spray the loaves with water. When you put the bread into the oven, drop several ice cubes into the cast-iron skillet to create steam.*
9. Bake for 20 minutes or until golden brown. Remove from oven, turn out of pans, if you use them, and cool on wire rack.
   *Note that steam can be damaging to some ovens, particularly the newer digitally controlled ovens.

Ingredients

For the starter, part 1:
- 1 cup warm water
- ½ teaspoon fresh yeast
- 1 cup buttermilk
- 1½ cups plain yogurt
- 2 cups white flour
- ⅓ cup semolina
- 1 cup grapes, cut in two and tied up in cheesecloth

For the starter, part 2:
- ½ teaspoon fresh yeast
- 2 cups warm water
- 2 cups white flour
- 1 cup semolina

For the dough:
- ¾ teaspoon fresh yeast
- ¾ cup warm water
- 1½ cups white flour
- 1½ cups whole wheat flour
- 1½ cups starter
- 1 tablespoon salt

Difficulty

Advanced

Preparation

8 hours and 1 day

Portion

2 loaves

GARLIC AND PARSLEY BREAD

This garlicky bread, swirled with fresh parsley, is both delicious and easy to make.

Preparation

1. Combine flour with sugar and salt. Mix well and stir in the yeast.
2. In a separate bowl, combine milk, eggs, and sour cream. Add wet ingredients to flour mixture. Beat at least 5 minutes.
3. Form two balls, cover, and let double in size, resting dough at least 2 hours.
4. Make the filling: heat the garlic in the oil without browning. (If you prefer the taste of raw garlic, you can leave raw.) Add parsley and stir.
5. Preheat oven to 425°F.
6. Stretch each ball of dough into a rectangle approximately 16 y 20 inches. Spread half of the filling over two-thirds of each. Roll up tightly, beginning at the long edge of the rectangle (see photo). Place on baking sheet that has been either greased and floured or lined with parchment paper. Let loaves rise 20 minutes.
7. Brush with egg white and bake until rolls begin to brown, approximately 25 to 30 minutes. Cool on wire rack.

Ingredients

- 4½ cups flour, plus extra
- ½ cup sugar
- 1 teaspoon salt
- 1 tablespoon instant yeast
- 1¼ cups warm milk
- 2 eggs
- ½ cup sour cream
- 1 egg white, beaten
  For the filling:
- ⅓ cup finely chopped fresh garlic
- ½ cup olive oil
- 1 cup finely chopped parsley

Difficulty

Easy to Intermediate

Preparation

4 hours

Portion

2 loaves

PESTO-FILLED BREAD

I love eating bread that has been made by my hands. Everything tastes better when it's homemade! If you don't care for pesto, simply leave it out.

   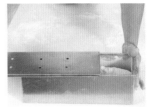

Preparation

1. Make the pesto: Combine all pesto ingredients in a food processor, process, and set aside.
2. Make the dough: Mix 6 cups of the flour with the salt, sugar, and yeast. Add the butter, shortening, and enough water or milk so that no flour remains loose (add a little at a time). Beat or knead for 8 minutes. Add remaining flour, as much or as little as is necessary to form a dough that is very soft and sticky but manageable.
3. Cut the dough into two pieces. Cover the dough, set in a warm place, and let rise until doubled in size, about 2 hours.
4. Roll out one piece of the dough to a rectangle of about 9 by 12 inches and spread evenly with pesto, using as much or as little as suits your taste. Roll tightly and fold ends of loaf over (see photo). Repeat with the other piece of dough.
5. Preheat oven to 375°F.
6. Place each bread in a loaf pan—preferably a Pullman loaf pan (which features a top, for producing perfectly square breads)—that has been greased and floured (fill no more than two-thirds of the pan). Grease and flour the top of the pan before fitting it onto the pan. Let rise 20 minutes more.
7. Bake about 40 minutes. Uncover (if using a Pullman pan) and bake until the top of the bread is golden brown, about 20 minutes more.

Ingredients

7	cups flour
1	tablespoon salt
3	tablespoons sugar
1½	tablespoons instant yeast
½	cup butter (1 stick)
3	tablespoons shortening
2¼	cups water or milk (or a bit more or less)

For pesto:

½	cup basil (leaves)
2	tablespoons Parmesan
2	cloves garlic
½	cup olive oil
	salt and pepper, to taste

Difficulty

Easy to Intermediate

Preparation

4 hours

Portion

2 loaves

BREAD STUFFED WITH ROASTED PEPPERS, WALNUTS, AND BASIL

This savory bread makes a perfect appetizer. Serve it with cheese and fine wine for a delightful start to any meal.

Ingredients

5	cups flour, plus extra
1	tablespoon instant yeast
1	teaspoon salt
2	tablespoons sugar
2	eggs
¼	cup vegetable oil
⅓	cup sour cream
	warm milk, as necessary
	olive oil, for brushing
	For the filling:
2	roasted red peppers, finely chopped
1	teaspoon Italian seasoning, plus extra for garnish
2	tablespoons olive oil
	salt and pepper, to taste
1	cup basil leaves, chopped
1	cup shredded mozzarella
1	cup walnuts, toasted and chopped

Preparation

1. Mix the flour with the yeast. Add salt, sugar, eggs, vegetable oil, and sour cream. Start adding milk until dough is soft and sticky. Beat 5 minutes in a stand mixer.
2. Place dough in a greased bowl, cover, and let rise at least 2 hours, or until it doubles in size.
3. Begin making the filling: Mix roasted red peppers with Italian seasoning, olive oil, salt, and pepper. Set aside.
4. Divide dough into six equal parts. Press the first portion of dough into the bottom of a greased and floured loaf pan. Repeat with two more pieces in two more pans.
5. Cover each piece of dough with a third of the pepper mixture and sprinkle with a third of the basil, cheese, and walnuts. Press another layer of dough over each bread. Let rise 30 minutes.
6. While bread is rising, preheat oven to 375°F.
7. Brush the tops of the dough generously with olive oil. Sprinkle with Italian seasoning.
8. Bake until golden, 25 to 30 minutes.

Difficulty

Intermediate

Preparation

3 hours

Portion

3 loaves

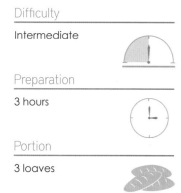

RUSTIC BREAD WITH DILL AND OREGANO

Oregano and dill are a terrific, though somewhat unusual, pairing. This country-style bread goes wonderfully with all sorts of fish dishes.

Preparation

1. Mix together the flour and yeast. Add salt, dill seed, and oregano. Add 1¾ cups water and mix, adding additional water as needed to form a sticky dough.
2. Beat for 6 to 8 minutes.
3. Place dough in an oiled plastic bag and let rest until dough has doubled in size, at least 3 hours.
4. Knead again, adding flour to make a stiff dough. Form into two large balls.
5. Place on a baking sheet that has been greased and floured or lined with parchment paper and let rise for about 30 minutes.
6. Preheat oven to 400°F. Place a cast-iron skillet on oven rack below the rack on which you'll be baking the bread.
7. Brush dough with water and sprinkle with enough flour to cover the bread. Make cuts to the tops of the loaves.
8. When you put the bread in the oven, drop several ice cubes into the cast-iron skillet to create steam.* Bake until the crust is golden and the loaves sound hollow when tapped on the bottom, 25 to 35 minutes.
   *Note that steam can be damaging to some ovens, particularly newer digitally controlled models.

Ingredients

4	cups flour (if possible, use bread flour), plus extra
2	tablespoons instant yeast
1	tablespoon salt
1	teaspoon dill seed
1	teaspoon dried oregano
1¾–2	cups water

Difficulty

Intermediate

Preparation

4 to 5 hours

Portion

2 loaves

CHALLAH

My nana, Ata, raised me, and I owe so much of my cooking skill to her. This is her special challah recipe.

   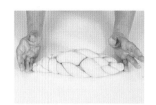

Preparation

1. Add yeast and 1 teaspoon of the sugar to ½ cup warm water. Let stand 10 minutes.
2. Mix flour with remaining sugar and salt.
3. In a separate bowl, beat eggs with oil and remaining water. Add wet ingredients to the flour mixture. Stir in yeast mixture.
4. Knead for approximately 8 minutes.
5. Cover dough and let rise until it doubles in size, 2 to 3 hours.
6. Preheat oven to 375°F.
7. Knead by hand (if you need to add a little flour, go ahead, but do not overdo it, as this is a soft bread).
8. Form six balls and stretch them, forming thick ropes that are thinner at the ends than in the center. Braid the ropes (see photo), and let rise 20 minutes, covered. If you have trouble braiding with six strands, form two braids of three!
9. Brush the bread with egg yolk beaten with 1 teaspoon milk and a pinch of salt, and bake until golden, 25 to 30 minutes.

Variation: Challah Stuffed with Cheese

1. Prepare the dough as for Challah, above.
2. Mix the two cheeses together in a food processor and process until smooth.
3. Add flour, egg yolks, salt, vanilla, and sugar to taste. If desired, add raisins and/or zest.
4. Once the dough has doubled in size, roll out to ¼ inch thick. Cut circles of about 2¼ inches in diameter and brush with beaten egg. Place a spoonful of the cheese filling in the center. Fold up the edges of each circle on three sides to form a triangle shape.
5. Brush with beaten egg and bake at 375°F until the triangles begin to brown.

Ingredients

2	tablespoons active dry yeast
¾	cup sugar
1½	cups warm water
5	cups flour, plus extra
1	teaspoon salt
4	eggs
¼	cup vegetable oil
1	egg yolk, beaten
1	teaspoon milk
	pinch of salt

Filling for Variation:

10½	ounces farmer's cheese
4	ounces cream cheese
3	tablespoons flour
2	egg yolks
	pinch of salt
1	tablespoon vanilla
⅔	cup sugar, or to taste
	raisins (optional)
	orange zest (optional)

Difficulty

Easy to Intermediate

Preparation

1 to 2 hours

Portion

1 to 2 loaves depending on size

BROWN BREAD WITH POPPY AND CARAWAY

I got the idea for this recipe many years ago, and it is still one of my favorites. It's a heavy, dark bread that goes perfectly with hearty fare like sausages.

Preparation

1. Mix the white flour and the whole grain wheat flour with the yeast. Add the seeds, walnuts, flax, and salt. Form a mound with a well in the center.
2. In a separate bowl, lightly beat the eggs. Add oil, buttermilk, honey, molasses, and 1 cup warm water to the beaten eggs and mix well.
3. Stir wet ingredients into the flour, adding more water as necessary until a very sticky dough forms. Cover with plastic wrap and let rise about 3 hours.
4. Punch down dough, adding a little more flour if necessary. Knead until dough is easy to handle, about 5 minutes.
5. Form two loaves and place them on greased and floured baking sheets or in standard loaf pans that have been well greased and floured. Make cuts at the top of the bread and let rise 30 minutes.
6. Preheat oven to 375°F.
7. Brush the loaves with water, sprinkle with seeds, and bake about 30 minutes. Remove from oven and cool on a wire rack

Ingredients

3   cups white flour, plus extra as needed
3   cups whole grain wheat flour
1½ tablespoons instant yeast
2   tablespoons caraway seeds, plus additional for sprinkling
2   tablespoons poppy seeds, plus additional for sprinkling
⅓   cup chopped toasted walnuts
¼   cup ground flax
1½ tablespoons salt
3   eggs
½   cup vegetable oil
1   cup buttermilk
⅓   cup honey
2   tablespoons molasses
1   cup warm water, plus additional as necessary

Difficulty

Easy to Intermediate

Preparation

3 to 4 hours

Portion

2 loaves

FRESH HERB BREAD

Scrumptious with any meal, this lovely herb-flavored bread pairs wonderfully with pasta, chicken, fish, or a delicious salad.

Ingredients

7	cups flour
1	tablespoon salt
½	cup sugar
2	tablespoons instant yeast
3	eggs, lightly beaten
½	cup (1 stick) butter, melted
½	cup oil
1½	cup milk
1	tablespoon each fresh herbs: tarragon, rosemary, basil, oregano, and sage
	water, as needed
¼	cup (½ stick) butter, melted, for brushing dough
¼	cup sesame seeds

Preparation

1. Mix together flour, salt, and sugar. Add yeast.
2. In a separate bowl, beat eggs, and add the butter, oil, herbs, and milk. Stir into the flour mixture.
3. Add more milk or water if needed to get a sticky dough.
4. Let dough rest at least 1 hour.
5. Knead the dough, adding a little more flour if needed to make it manageable, and let rise 2 hours.
6. Preheat oven to 375°F.
7. Form dough into three or four loaves, and place them 2 inches apart on a baking sheet that has been greased and floured or lined with parchment paper. Brush with melted butter and sprinkle with sesame seeds.
8. Bake the loaves until they begin to brown, 25 to 30 minutes.

Difficulty

Easy

Preparation

3 hours

Portion

3 loaves

PEPPERY CHEESE BREAD

Resplendent with Parmesan and freshly ground black pepper, this bread is wonderful served with a robust wine, aged cheeses, and prosciutto.

Preparation

1. Mix together flour, pepper, Parmesan (with a tablespoon reserved for sprinkling), salt, and sugar. Add yeast and stir well.
2. In a separate bowl, mix egg and oil with 1 cup warm water. Add to the flour mixture. Keep adding water until the dough is sticky.
3. Beat on medium speed 5 minutes.
4. Cover dough tightly with plastic wrap and let rise 2 to 3 hours. Punch dough down.
5. Preheat oven to 350°F.
6. Form a round loaf and place it in a 14-inch round pan that has been greased and floured. Make slits in the top of the dough with a sharp knife. Brush with egg white and sprinkle with reserved Parmesan and extra pepper.
7. Let rise 20 minutes.
8. Bake until golden, 30 to 40 minutes.

Ingredients

4	cups flour
1–2	teaspoons ground black pepper, to taste
¾	cup Parmesan (reserve a tablespoon for sprinkling)
1	teaspoon salt
1	tablespoon sugar
1	tablespoon instant yeast
1	egg (reserve 1 teaspoon of the white to brush the bread)
3	tablespoons vegetable oil
1	cup warm water, plus more as needed

Difficulty

Easy to Intermediate

Preparation

4 to 5 hours

Portion

1 loaf

FIVE GRAIN BREAD

This hearty bread is full of fiber, perfect for a healthy breakfast when toasted.

Preparation

1. Make the dough starter (sponge): combine the 2 cups water, 1 cup flour, and 1 tablespoon yeast and let stand at least 5 to 6 hours at room temperature.
2. Make the dough: Mix the whole wheat and white flour with the yeast, salt, cocoa, barley, rolled oats, flax seeds, poppy seeds, and walnuts.
3. In a separate bowl, combine the dough starter with the water, honey, molasses, and oil and beat until dough is fluffy. It will be sticky.
4. Continue beating 8 minutes. Let rise until doubled in size, about 3 to 4 hours.
5. Preheat oven to 425°F. Place cast-iron skillet on oven rack below the rack on which you'll be baking the bread.
6. Form dough into two balls and place on baking sheets that have been greased and floured or lined with parchment paper. Make several cuts across top of each loaf with a sharp knife.
7. Brush each loaf with water and sprinkle with oats. When you put the bread into the oven, drop several ice cubes into the cast-iron skillet to create steam.* Bake for 10 minutes.
8. After the bread has baked for 10 minutes, turn the oven down to 375°F and finish baking, about 30 more minutes. *Note that steam can be damaging to some ovens, particularly newer digitally controlled models.

Ingredients

For the dough starter (sponge):

2 cups water
1 cup flour
1 tablespoon instant yeast

For the dough:

3¾ cups whole wheat flour
3 cups white flour
1 tablespoon instant yeast
2 teaspoons salt
1 tablespoon pure cocoa
¾ cup barley, soaked in water a few hours
1½ cups rolled oats
½ cup flax seeds
½ cup poppy seeds
1 cup chopped toasted walnuts
2¾ cups warm water, plus additional, if necessary
⅓ cup honey
1 tablespoon molasses
3 tablespoons vegetable oil
oats, for garnish

Difficulty

Easy

Preparation

10 hours

Portion

2 loaves

47

BASIL SPIRAL BREAD

This basil-laced bread has the taste of the garden about it—fresh and delicious.

Ingredients

1	teaspoon sugar
2½	teaspoons granulated dry yeast
½	cup warm water, plus more as needed
3¼	cups of bread flour, plus extra as needed
⅓	cup light olive oil
1	small egg
1	teaspoon salt
	olive oil, for brushing bread

For the filling:

2	cups fresh basil leaves, washed, dried, and finely chopped
2	tablespoons light olive oil

Difficulty

Easy

Preparation

3 to 4 hours

Portion

1 loaf

Preparation

1. Dissolve sugar and yeast in the warm water and let stand 10 minutes.
2. Place flour, oil, egg, yeast mixture, and salt in the bowl of a stand mixer. Beat 6 minutes. If dough seems dry during mixing (if all flour is not incorporated), add more water as needed.
3. Place the dough in a greased bowl and let double in size, about 2 hours.
4. Punch down dough. Roll dough into a rectangular shape 8 inches by 16 inches. Brush with plenty of olive oil. Spread the basil leaves over the rectangle, and roll tightly.
5. Preheat oven to 375°F.
6. Place dough in a greased and floured ring-shaped pan. Cover and let stand 20 minutes. Brush with olive oil and bake until top begins to brown, 30 to 40 minutes.

BASIL-AND-CHEESE-FILLED BREAD

This scrumptious bread is a bit like a stuffed pizza, filled with garden-fresh basil and yummy mozzarella.

Preparation

1. Mix flour, salt, and sugar. Stir the yeast into the flour mixture and form mound with a well in the middle. Add the melted butter and warm milk to the well, starting with ½ cup and adding milk slowly until all flour is incorporated. Mix until dough forms, about 7 minutes in stand mixer or 12 minutes by hand. The dough will be compact.
2. Divide the dough into two balls. Cover with plastic wrap and let rise 2 to 3 hours.
3. Meanwhile, make the filling: Mash the onions with the olive oil and salt, squeezing well to get rid of the liquid. Combine with basil.
4. Preheat oven to 400°F.
5. Generously oil a 14-inch to 16-inch round baking pan. Roll out or stretch one piece of the dough until it fits into the bottom of the pan.
6. Brush the surface of the dough with olive oil and top with mozzarella and onion mixture. Stretch the other piece of dough to cover the filling. Press with your fingers to seal edges well all around. Cut a hole in the center of the top and press down to release any trapped air. Let rise 20 minutes.
7. Brush the top of the bread with water and sift flour over the surface. Bake until golden, 35 to 40 minutes.

Ingredients

- 5 cups flour, plus extra
- 1 teaspoon salt
- ¼ cup sugar
- 1 tablespoon instant yeast
- ¼ cup melted butter
- ½ cup warm milk, plus more as necessary

For the filling:

- 2 onions, cut julienne
- 2 tablespoons olive oil, plus extra for brushing
- 1 tablespoon salt
- 30 fresh basil leaves, chopped
- 2¼ cups mozzarella

Difficulty

Intermediate

Preparation

4 to 5 hours

Portion

1 round loaf

FOCACCIA STUFFED WITH OLIVES

A flat-topped Italian bread, focaccia is delicious and easy to make at home! This recipe incorporates fragrant olives for a glorious taste of sunny Italy

Preparation

1. Make the dough starter: combine the yeast and the milk. Stir well and mix with the 1¼ cups flour. Cover with plastic wrap and let rise for at least 30 minutes.
2. Make the dough: mix together all dough ingredients. Combine the dough starter with the all of the dough ingredients. Knead in a stand mixer or hand knead just until the dough is smooth. Oil the inside of a large food-safe plastic bag designed for cooking (such as for sous vide) and place dough inside. Press all air from the bag and seal or knot the top.
3. On low heat, warm a pot of water large enough to hold the bag of dough. Place the bag in the water. Let dough ferment 1½ hours.
4. Preheat oven to 375°F.
5. Mix filling ingredients together and set aside.
6. Cut the dough in half and stretch each piece into a rectangle about 8 by 11 inches.
7. Cover the middle two-thirds of each rectangle with the filling. Fold the dough over in three parts, as if you are folding a letter to go into an envelope. Take care to seal the edges well. Place on baking sheets that have been greased and floured or lined with parchment paper.
8. Drizzle the top of each of the focaccia with olive oil and press with fingers to dimple the dough.
9. Bake for 20 to 25 minutes.

Ingredients

For the dough starter (sponge):
2 tablespoons granulated dry yeast
1 cup milk
1¼ cups flour
For the dough:
3 cups flour
1 tablespoon sugar
1 teaspoon salt
pepper, to taste
⅓ cup water
1½ ounces butter, softened
¼ cup olive oil, plus extra for drizzling
½ cup milk, plus more as needed
For the filling:
1½ cup sliced black olives
2 tablespoons olive oil
1 cup good-quality Parmesan
1 cup finely chopped chives
2 red onions, julienned

Difficulty

Intermediate

Preparation

4 hours

Portion

2 focaccia

GARLIC AND ROSEMARY FOCACCIA

This delightful version of a classic Italian bread is fragrant with garlic and fresh rosemary.

Preparation

1. Combine flour, Italian seasoning, yeast, and sugar in a stand mixer or by hand.
2. In a separate bowl, stir together the water, olive oil, and salt. Add to flour mixture, whisking gently (if you need more water, add at this time, until the mix forms a sticky dough).
3. Mix about 5 minutes or until dough is smooth. Cut dough in half and form into two balls. Cover tightly with plastic wrap and let dough rest until it doubles in size, about 45 minutes.
4. Preheat oven to 450°F.
5. Roll each piece of dough into a circle about ½ inch. Place on a greased and floured baking sheet. Let stand 10 minutes.
6. Meanwhile, caramelize the garlic in olive oil, seasoning with the salt and pepper. Take care not to burn the garlic. Set aside.
7. Brush the focaccia with olive oil and bake about 8 minutes, or longer if you like yours crispier.
8. Once the focaccia is baked, spread the caramelized garlic over the top and sprinkle with fresh rosemary, coarse salt, and pepper. Sprinkle with Parmesan. Serve warm.

Ingredients

3½–4 cups flour
1 teaspoon Italian seasoning
2 teaspoons instant yeast
2 tablespoons sugar
1 cup warm water, plus extra as needed
3 tablespoons olive oil
1 tablespoon salt
For the topping:
olive oil, for cooking garlic
10–12 cloves garlic, minced
1 tablespoon large-grained salt (such as coarse sea salt), or to taste
black pepper, to taste
2 tablespoons fresh rosemary
¼ cup grated Parmesan

Difficulty

Easy to Intermediate

Preparation

2 hours

Portion

2 focaccia

FOCACCIA WITH ROASTED TOMATO AND BASIL SAUCE

A fabulous alternative to garlic bread, this focaccia recipe features two of the signature flavors of Italy—tomatoes and basil.

Preparation

1. To make the sauce: Preheat oven to 450°F. Line a baking sheet with parchment paper. Wash the tomatoes and split them in half, and place on the baking sheet cut sides down. Scatter the onion on the baking sheet. Cut the heads of garlic in half and place on the baking sheet. Drizzle the vegetables with olive oil and sprinkle with Italian herbs, salt and pepper, and cayenne. Roast until tomatoes and onions are beginning to darken, about 25 to 30 minutes.
2. Once vegatables are roasted, let them cool slightly. Peel the roasted garlic and place in a food processor, along with tomatoes, onions, herbs, and the broth. Blend for a few minutes. You can strain the sauce if you like, but I love the chunky texture of the unstrained sauce.
3. Cook in a saucepan over medium heat for about 20 minutes or until reduced by about half. Season to taste with more salt and pepper if needed, add sugar, and sprinkle with finely chopped basil.
4. Make the focaccia: Combine the flour, sugar, and salt. Mix well and add the yeast.
5. In a separate bowl, beat egg with 2 tablespoons olive oil and ½ cup warm water. Add the flour mixture and keep adding water until dough is easy to handle.
6. Place in a covered bowl and let rise until doubled in size, about 2 hours.
7. Punch down dough, and roll or stretch into a rectangle of about 18 by 24 inches. Place on a baking sheet greased with olive oil.
8. Preheat oven to 450°F.
9. Let rise 20 minutes. Brush with extra-virgin olive oil and season with salt, pepper, and Italian herbs, to taste.
10. Bake for 20 minutes.
11. When focaccia is ready, brush with additional olive oil and spread with tomato sauce.

Ingredients

For the sauce:
5 pounds plum tomatoes
2 onions, cut into thick slices
2 whole heads of garlic
olive oil, for drizzling
salt and pepper, to taste
fresh Italian herbs (rosemary, oregano, sage, marjoram), for sprinkling
cayenne pepper, to taste
6 cups chicken or vegetable broth
1 tablespoon sugar
1 large bunch of basil, stems and all (at least 40 leaves), finely chopped
For the focaccia:
3 cups flour, plus extra
1 teaspoon sugar
1 tablespoon salt
1 tablespoon instant yeast
1 small egg
2 tablespoons olive oil
½ cup warm water, plus more as necessary
extra-virgin olive oil, for brushing
salt and pepper, to taste
fresh Italian herbs (rosemary, oregano, sage, marjoram), for sprinkling

Difficulty

Intermediate

Preparation

4 to 5 hours

Portion

2 focaccia

PIZZA BREAD

This savory bread, filled with the flavors of Italy, makes a fantastic appetizer.

Ingredients

3½	cups flour
1	tablespoon instant yeast
1	teaspoon salt
2	tablespoons sugar
¼	cup melted butter
½	cup water, plus more as needed

For the filling:

2	onions, chopped
2	red bell peppers, chopped
1	small eggplant, peeled and chopped
1	zucchini, chopped
1½	cups basic tomato sauce (or more or less, to taste)
2–3	cups shredded mozzarella Italian herbs (for sprinkling)

Preparation

1. In a bowl, mix the flour and yeast well. Add salt and sugar, and stir. Mix melted butter with ½ cup water and continue stirring. Add more water, as needed, until all loose flour disappears.
2. Knead about 10 minutes. Let dough rise until doubled in size, about 2 hours.
3. Punch down dough, and roll out or stretch to a rectangle of about 20 by 24 inches.
4. Mix together onion, bell pepper, eggplant, and zucchini. Spread dough with tomato sauce, vegetable mixture, and mozzarella to taste.
5. Sprinkle with Italian herbs and wrap tightly to form a roll.
6. Place seam side down on a baking sheet that has been greased and floured or lined with parchment paper.
7. Preheat oven to 375°F.
8. Make several cuts in the top of dough to vent, and let rise 30 minutes.
9. Bake until the bread begins to brown, 30 to 40 minutes. Serve hot or warm.

Difficulty

Intermediate

Preparation

3 to 4 hours

Portion

1 large loaf

OLIVE BREAD

Mediterranean olives make this rustic bread an ideal pairing with cream cheese and salmon—what a treat for lunch or with evening cocktails.

Ingredients

2¼–2¾	cups white flour
2	cups whole wheat flour
1	tablespoon sugar
1	tablespoon salt
2	tablespoons instant yeast
½	cup vegetable oil
2	eggs
1	cup milk
	warm water as needed
4	ounces hard cheese, such as grated Parmesan or Asiago or crumbled feta
½	cup sliced black olives

Preparation

1. Mix together white flour, whole wheat flour, sugar, salt, and yeast.
2. In a separate bowl, mix together oil, eggs, and milk. Add to the flour mixture. Add water until dough is smooth but sticky. Cover and let rise 2 to 3 hours.
3. Knead well, about 5 to 7 minutes. Add cheese and olives, mixing until well incorporated.
4. Preheat oven to 375°F.
5. Form one large loaf and let rise 30 minutes.
6. Bake until golden, about 25 minutes.

Difficulty

Easy to Intermediate

Preparation

3 to 4 hours

Portion

1 loaf

ROLLS & OTHER SAVORY YEAST BREADS

Parker House Rolls • Doris's Rolls • Dinner Rolls • Herbed Rolls • Yogurt Rolls
Hamburger and Hotdog Rolls • Potato Sourdough Loaves • Chive Rolls
Bonnet Rolls • Cheese Rolls • Onion Bread • Fugazza • Bagels • Middle
Eastern Flatbread • Sesame Rings • Poppy Seed and Onion Spirals • Buns
with Caraway • English Muffins • Pita Bread • Crispy Breadsticks • Soda
Breadsticks • Zucchini-Filled Ring

PARKER HOUSE ROLLS

These buttery rolls are a classic, and have been a dinnertime favorite for more than a century. A friend gave me this version of the recipe many years ago—it's delicious!

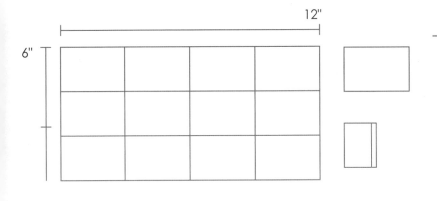

Ingredients

1	tablespoon active dry yeast
¼	cup warm water
1	cup milk
¼	cup shortening
3	tablespoons sugar
2	teaspoons salt
1	large egg
3½	cups flour
¼	cup melted butter
	coarse salt, to taste

Preparation

1. Place yeast in ¼ cup warm water, stir well, and let dissolve 5 to 7 minutes. Set aside.
2. Heat milk, then remove from burner. Cut the shortening into small pieces and add to the hot milk a little at a time, stirring constantly until the shortening melts.
3. Add sugar and salt to the milk and shortening mixture and stir well. Add the yeast mixture, egg, and flour, stirring to combine. Knead dough until smooth, about 15 minutes by hand or 10 minutes in a stand mixer. Cover and let stand 2 hours.
4. Preheat oven to 350°F.
5. Melt ¼ cup butter and use it to thoroughly grease a 13-by-9-inch pan. Reserve the rest of the melted butter for brushing rolls.
6. Divide dough into two parts.
7. Roll each piece of dough into a 6-by-12-inch rectangle and cut into three strips 2 inches wide. Cut each strip into four pieces, 2 by 3 inches each. Stretch rectangle a bit.
8. Brush each with melted butter and fold almost in half, leaving part uncovered. Repeat with all the dough. Place rolls on baking sheets lined with parchment paper.
9. Brush rolls with butter and refrigerate at least 30 minutes or up to 6 hours. Bake for 20 to 25 minutes. When rolls come out of the oven, brush again with melted butter and sprinkle with coarse salt.

Difficulty

Intermediate

Preparation

4 hours

Portion

24 rolls

DORIS'S ROLLS

One of my fondest memories is the sound of my children's voices calling from upstairs, "Ma, are the rolls out of the oven yet?" While the rolls were still warm, we'd sit down to savor them with sweet butter!

Preparation

1. Make dough starter (sponge): Stir together 3½ cups of the flour, yeast, sugar, and salt.
2. Add 1¾ cups water to the mix, stir with a wooden spoon, and let rest for 30 minutes, covered.
3. Mix the dough: Mix 3 eggs and oil together until fluffy, either whisking by hand or with a stand mixer.
4. Mix the dough starter with the egg and oil mixture, adding the remaining flour. Knead until a smooth dough forms. The dough should be somewhat sticky or gluey (if you need more water, add it).
5. Cover and let stand 2 hours in a warm place.
6. Grease and flour three baking sheets.
7. Knead again, then form the dough into 36 rolls (depending on the size and shape you want them) and place them about ½ inch apart on the baking sheets. The rolls may be formed by making slightly flattened balls (this is simplest) or by rolling a piece of dough into a long log, then folding it in half, twisting, and tucking the double end of the twist through the loop (see photos). Make sure to place rolls of different shapes on separate baking sheets, as larger rolls will take longer to bake.
8. Cover the rolls with plastic wrap and let stand 30 minutes.
9. While dough is rising, preheat oven to 400°F.
10. Brush the rolls lightly with beaten egg and sprinkle with seeds.
11. Bake until the rolls are golden brown and sound hollow when tapped on the bottom, about 20 to 25 minutes.
12. Cool on a wire rack.

    Variations:

    (After completing step 9, instead of using seeds)
    · Spread tops of dough with jam. Brush with beaten egg and sprinkle with sugar before baking.
    · Stir together cinnamon, sugar, toasted walnuts, and raisins. Brush each roll with beaten egg and sprinkle with the mixture before baking.
    · Brush rolls with beaten egg and sprinkle with cheese, to taste.
    · Add cheese to dough. Brush top with beaten egg and sprinkle with the seeds of your choice.

Ingredients

For the dough starter (sponge):
3½ cups flour
2 tablespoons instant yeast
½ cup sugar
2 teaspoons salt
1¾ cups water, plus additional as needed
For the dough:
3 eggs
½ cup vegetable oil
3½ cups flour
1 egg, beaten
For variations:
⅓ cup jam
⅓ cup cinnamon
1 cup sugar
1 cup chopped toasted walnuts
1 cup raisins
2 cups cheddar
poppy, caraway, and sesame seeds, for sprinkling

Difficulty

Easy to Intermediate

Preparation

4 hours

Portion

36 rolls

DINNER ROLLS

Simple and comforting, these classic dinner rolls are an ideal accompaniment to any meal—meat, chicken, or fish.

Preparation

1. Mix ½ cup milk with eggs, ¼ cup butter, oil, sugar, and salt.
2. Mix flour and yeast together, then stir in the milk and eggs mixture. Add more milk if necessary to make a sticky dough. Beat the dough 5 to 7 minutes.
3. Let rise 2 to 3 hours. Form balls the size of a walnut and place them ½ inch apart on a greased and floured baking sheet. Let rise 30 minutes.
4. While rolls are rising, preheat oven to 400°F.
5. Brush rolls with melted butter, sprinkle with seeds and bake for 15 to 20 minutes. Cool on a wire rack.

Ingredients

- ½ cup milk, plus more as needed
- 2 eggs
- ¼ cup melted butter
- 2 tablespoons vegetable oil
- 3 tablespoons sugar
- 1 teaspoon salt
- 4 cups flour
- 1 tablespoon instant yeast
  melted butter, for brushing
  sesame seeds, for sprinkling

Difficulty

Easy

Preparation

3 to 4 hours

Portion

48 rolls

HERBED ROLLS

Fresh herbs and a soft interior make these rolls a delicious addition to dinnertime!

Preparation

1. Stir together flour, yeast, salt, and sugar, and form a mound with a well in the middle.
2. In a separate bowl, combine eggs, sour cream, herbs, and minced garlic. Mix well, then pour into the well of the flour mixture and stir to combine.
3. Knead, adding ¾ cup milk; add additional milk as necessary to yield a sticky but manageable dough.
4. Place dough in a greased bowl, cover with bread cloth or plastic wrap, and let rise for 2 hours.
5. Roll dough into 20 to 24 balls, depending on the size you want your rolls, and place at least 1 inch apart on a greased and floured baking sheet.
6. Allow 30 minutes for the dough to rise again. While dough is rising, preheat oven to 400°F.
7. Brush rolls with melted butter and bake for 20 to 25 minutes.

Ingredients

3½	cups flour
2	teaspoons instant yeast
1	tablespoon salt
2	teaspoons sugar
2	eggs
½	cup sour cream
2	tablespoons chopped fresh basil
1	tablespoon chopped fresh rosemary
1	tablespoon chopped fresh sage
1	tablespoon chopped fresh mint
1	clove garlic, minced
¾–1¼	cups milk, as necessary melted butter, for brushing

Difficulty

Intermediate

Preparation

3½ hours

Portion

20 to 24 rolls

YOGURT ROLLS

These delectable rolls are perfect for a light breakfast... simply delicious!

Preparation

1. Combine 4 cups of the flour with the salt and sugar. Stir well, then add the yeast. Mix all together.
2. Add to the dry ingredients the yogurt, egg, and 1 cup milk, plus additional milk as necessary to form a sticky dough.
3. Place dough in a greased bowl, cover, and set in a warm place. Let dough rest until it doubles in size, at least 2 hours.
4. Punch down dough to release the gas and knead, adding the remaining ½ cup of flour, until the dough is elastic and manageable. Do not add too much flour; the dough should be soft. Knead well for at least 5 minutes.
5. Form rolls by pulling or cutting dough into 20 to 24 pieces. Roll each piece into a long rope and tie in a loose knot; tuck both ends under roll and stretch knot slightly to form long roll. Place ½ inch apart on baking sheets lined with parchment paper.
6. Cover with plastic wrap or bread cloth and let stand 20 minutes. While dough is resting, preheat oven to 400°F.
7. Sift flour on top of each roll and bake until golden, about 18 to 20 minutes. Cool on a wire rack.

Ingredients

4½	cups flour, plus extra as needed
1	teaspoon salt
1	tablespoon sugar
1½	tablespoons instant yeast
⅔	cup plain yogurt
1	egg
1–1½	cups milk, as necessary (skim milk can be used if desired)

Difficulty

Easy to Intermediate

Preparation

4 hours

Portion

20 to 24 rolls

HAMBURGER AND HOTDOG ROLLS

Take the time to make these fantastic rolls for your next backyard barbecue—you are sure to get rave reviews!

Ingredients

8	cups flour
5	teaspoons salt
4½	tablespoons sugar
⅓	cup butter
2	teaspoons malt extract
2½	tablespoons powdered milk
2¼	cups water
3	tablespoons yeast

Preparation

1. Combine all ingredients and knead until dough is silky and elastic, 10 to 12 minutes
2. Let rest 10 minutes.
3. Cut dough in half. Take half the dough, and cut into 10 to 12 equally sized pieces. Form them into balls and press down on the top, until they are flattened into rounds of 3 to 3½ inches each. Take the other half of the dough and cut into 10 to 12 equally sized pieces. Roll them into logs of about 6 inches in length. Place the hamburger and hotdog rolls about 3 inches apart on baking sheets that have been greased and floured or lined with parchment paper. Cover and let rise until tripled in size, 2 to 3 hours.
4. Preheat oven to 400°F.
5. Bake 20 to 25 minutes. Cool on a wire rack.
6.

Difficulty

Easy

Preparation

4 hours

Portion

20–24 rolls

POTATO SOURDOUGH LOAVES

Part potato bread, part sourdough bread, these little loaves are an amazing combination of two classics.

Preparation

1. Make the starter: The day before you plan to make the bread, combine all ingredients on starter list in a glass bowl, cover, and let sit overnight at room temperature.
2. Make the dough: Mix flour and semolina with yeast and salt. Set aside.
3. In a separate bowl, combine all 4 cups of the reserved potato water with molasses, honey, eggs, oil, and 1 cup starter.
4. Mash the potatoes, then stir the rest of the ingredients into them. The dough should be sticky but firm. If you need more water, add it now.
5. Place in a large plastic bag that has been well oiled, squeeze all air from the bag, and knot or seal the top.
6. Allow dough to double in size, about 3 to 5 hours.
7. Preheat oven to 325°F.
8. Punch down dough and divide the dough into ten balls.
9. Dip each ball in flour and place on a baking sheet lined with parchment paper. Cut a slit in the top of each ball.
10. Bake 30 to 35 minutes.

Ingredients

For the dough starter (sponge):
- 1 cup flour
- ½ teaspoon instant yeast
- ⅔ cup plain yogurt
- ½ cup buttermilk
- 1 cup warm water

For the dough:
- 6 cups flour, plus extra
- 1 cup semolina
- 1 tablespoon instant yeast
- 1 tablespoon salt
- 2¼ pounds unpeeled potatoes, cooked in 4 cups water (reserve the water)
- 2 tablespoons molasses
- ½ cup honey
- 3 eggs
- ⅓ cup vegetable oil
- 1 cup starter

Difficulty

Intermediate

Preparation

6 hours and 1 day

Portion

10 small loaves

CHIVE ROLLS

Chives impart a delicate onion flavor to these rolls, which are zkept moist with creamy cottage cheese and yogurt.

Preparation

1. Mix together flour, baking soda, and instant yeast. Stir well.
2. In a separate bowl, mix together oil, cottage cheese, and yogurt, then add salt, sugar, chives, and eggs, stirring to combine.
3. Add the wet ingredients to the dry ingredients and mix well. Add milk slowly, just until the mixture forms a sticky dough. Beat well for 8 minutes.
4. Cover the dough with plastic wrap and let rise 3 hours.
5. Punch down dough, knead, and form into balls, approximately 24 to 36 depending on the size you want your rolls. Place the rolls about 1 inch apart on a tray lined with parchment paper and let rise 30 minutes.
6. While rolls are rising, preheat oven to 350°F.
7. Brush the tops of rolls with butter and bake until golden, 20 to 25 minutes. Cool on a wire rack.

Ingredients

6	cups flour
½	teaspoon baking soda
2	tablespoons instant yeast
¼	cup vegetable oil
8	ounces cottage cheese
⅔	cup plain yogurt
2	teaspoons salt
¼	cup sugar
½	cup finely chopped chives
2	eggs
1	cup warm milk, approxmately
1	ounce (¼ stick) butter, melted

Difficulty

Easy to Intermediate

Preparation

4 hours

Portion

24 to 36 rolls

BONNET ROLLS

Walnuts give exquisite flavor to these little rolls. When you bite into them—mmmm—the textures make them truly unique.

Ingredients

4–4½ cups flour
1½ tablespoons instant yeast
1 teaspoon salt
2 tablespoons sugar
black pepper, to taste
⅓ cup butter, softened
1 teaspoon vegetable oil
warm water, as needed
1 cup chopped toasted walnuts

Preparation

1. Mix flour, yeast, salt, sugar, and pepper in the bowl of a mixer.
2. Add butter, oil, and a little water until dough is smooth and soft.
3. Beat for 5 minutes, then stir in the walnuts.
4. Cover and let rise about 3 hours.
5. Preheat oven to 375°F.
6. Roll out or stretch dough into a rectangle, about 8 by 16 inches. Cut into sixteen 1-inch-wide strips. Cut each strip in half, then tie the pieces into loose knots, forming a "bonnet" shape.
7. Place rolls 1 inch apart on a baking sheet lined with parchment paper. Bake 20 to 22 minutes, until the rolls sound hollow when tapped on the bottom.

Difficulty

Easy

Preparation

4 to 5 hours

Portion

32 rolls

CHEESE ROLLS

These delightful little rolls are so rich and cheesy... your family will be fighting over the crumbs!

Preparation

1. Mix together flour and instant yeast. Add sugar and salt to the flour mixture and stir well.
2. Melt butter and shortening and combine with the flour. Add all remaining ingredients, except the cheese, mixing well.
3. The dough should be sticky; if you need more buttermilk, add it. Beat 8 minutes. Place in a greased bowl and let double in size, about 2 to 3 hours.
4. Punch down dough. Add the cheese and knead lightly to combine. Cut into approximately 30 pieces. Roll the dough between your hands and a lightly floured surface to form ropes; tie the ropes into knots, tucking the ends underneath the roll. Place the rolls on greased and floured baking sheets, ½ inch apart.
5. Cover with plastic wrap and let rise 30 minutes. While the rolls are rising, preheat oven to 375°F.
6. Bake until golden, about 20 to 25 minutes. Remove to a wire rack to cool.

Ingredients

5	cups flour
1½	tablespoons instant yeast
¼	cup sugar
1	teaspoon salt
2	ounces (½ stick) butter
½	cup shortening
2	eggs
1½	cups buttermilk (more, as necessary)
1¼	cups grated semi-hard cheese, such as Colby, provolone, or Edam
1¼	cups shredded cheddar

Difficulty
Easy to Intermediate

Preparation
4 hours

Portion
30 rolls

ONION BREAD

Sautéed onions add sweetness to these fluffy little gems.

Preparation

1. Mix together shortening, sugar, salt, and 1½ cups warm water and heat over low heat until combined. Let mixture cool and add the egg.
2. In a separate bowl, mix the yeast and flour well. Combine with the mixture of warm water and egg. If you need more water, add at this time. The dough should be sticky.
3. Knead for several minutes.
4. Place the dough in a greased bowl, cover it, and let it rise about 2 to 3 hours.
5. While the dough is rising, cook the onion in oil on low, just until it is turning clear. Season with salt and pepper, and set aside.
6. Knead the dough for a few minutes, using more flour if needed. Roll into 24 to 30 balls the size of a walnut and let stand about 5 minutes.
7. Preheat oven to 325°F
8. Stretch balls into circles of about 2 inches, brush with egg, top with onions, and brush again with more egg white. Place on a greased and floured baking sheet about ½ inch apart. Let rise again for 15 minutes.
9. Bake until golden, about 20 minutes. Cool on a wire rack.

Ingredients

- ⅓ cup shortening
- 1 tablespoon sugar
- 1 tablespoon salt
- 1½–2 cups warm water, plus additional, if needed
- 1 egg
- 2 tablespoons instant yeast
- 4½ cups flour, plus extra
- 3 onions, finely chopped
    vegetable oil
    salt and pepper, to taste
- 1 egg, beaten

Difficulty

Easy to Intermediate

Preparation

4 hours

Portion

24 to 30 rolls

FUGAZZA

Fugazza is an airy, flat South American bread similar to focaccia or pizza. Instead of tomato sauce, fugazza is usually topped with savory sautéed onions.

 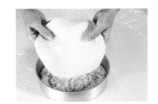  

Preparation

1. Mix onions, 1 tablespoon salt, and oil for topping in a bowl. Set aside.
2. For the dough, mix flour with the salt and sugar. Stir in the yeast and shape the mixture into a mound with a well in the center. Place the remaining dough ingredients in the center of the mound and mix well until a chewy dough forms. Knead well, until dough is smooth and elastic, about 15 minutes.
3. Cut the dough into four balls. Cover tightly with plastic and let rise until doubled in size, about 2 to 3 hours.
4. While the dough is rising, make the flavored oil: heat the olive oil with garlic and herbs (do not allow to boil). Set aside.
5. Squeeze the onion mixture until it releases as much liquid as possible. Discard the liquid.
6. Preheat oven to 375°F.
7. Oil two pizza pans with olive oil. Stretch one dough ball into a circle the size of the pizza pan, or place the dough in the pan and press it to fit. Top with half the grated mozzarella. Stretch another dough ball into the same-size circle and cover the "pizza," sealing the edges well by pinching with your fingers.
8. Make a little hole in the center of the pie and press down on the fugazza to remove all trapped air.
9. Repeat the steps above with the other two balls of dough.
10. Top each fugazza with onion mixture and salt and pepper to taste, and sprinkle with herbs.
11. Bake until golden, about 30 to 40 minutes. After removing from the oven, brush with the flavored olive oil.

Ingredients

For the topping and filling:
- 3 onions, julienned
- 1 tablespoon salt
- 2 tablespoon olive oil
- 14 ounces grated mozzarella, or to taste
- salt and pepper to taste
- Italian herbs for sprinkling, preferably fresh: basil, oregano rosemary, and thyme

For the dough and filling:
- 7 cups flour
- 1 tablespoon salt
- 2 tablespoons sugar
- 1 tablespoon instant yeast
- ¼ cup olive oil
- 2–2½ cups warm water

For flavored oil:
- ½ cup olive oil
- 1 tablespoon minced garlic
- 1 tablespoon fresh Italian herbs, such as basil, oregano, rosemary, and thyme

Difficulty

Intermediate

Preparation

4 hours

Portion

2 fugazza

BAGELS

There's no better breakfast than a fresh bagel topped with smoked salmon, cream cheese, and chives. . . . however, bagel and schmear has been known to be appreciated at any hour of the day!

Preparation

1. Combine 5 cups of the flour and the yeast. Add sugar and salt, and stir.
2. In a separate bowl, mix oil with water. Add the flour and yeast mixture to make a sticky dough. Knead at least 8 minutes at medium speed. Continue adding flour until dough is slightly more compact. Cover and let dough rise at least 3 hours in the refrigerator.
3. While the dough is rising, cook the onion on low in a tablespoon of oil; season with salt and pepper, and set aside. If you want seeds mixed in with the onion, add some now.
4. Preheat oven to 400°F.
5. Divide the dough into 24 equal portions. Form the dough into rings and let rise 30 minutes.
6. Bring a large pot of water to a boil, and add the tablespoon of sugar and ½ teaspoon of baking soda. Drop the bagels into the boiling water in pairs, cooking 20 seconds per side. Let each bagel drain on a spatula as you remove it from the water.
7. Carefully place bagels on a baking sheet lined with parchment paper. Brush with beaten egg white and top with the onion mixture. Sprinkle the bagels with sesame seeds, poppy seeds, caraway seeds, or rolled oats, if desired.
8. Bake until golden brown, about 20 minutes.

Ingredients

For the dough:
6 cups flour
2 tablespoons instant yeast
3 tablespoons sugar
1 teaspoon salt
1 tablespoon vegetable oil
2 cups warm water (approximately)
For the filling:
1 cup finely minced onion
1 tablespoon oil
salt and pepper, to taste
2 tablespoons each, sesame, poppy, and caraway seeds, or rolled oats (optional)
1 tablespoon sugar
½ teaspoon baking soda
1 egg white, beaten with
2 tablespoons water

Difficulty

Intermediate

Preparation

5 hours

Portion

24 bagels

MIDDLE EASTERN FLATBREAD

This tasty flatbread is a great accompaniment for dips, soups, and salads—or perfect enjoyed alone . . .

Ingredients

3   cups flour
½   teaspoon instant yeast
1   teaspoon salt
1   cup warm water (more as needed)
1   tablespoon vegetable oil
1   onion, grated or finely chopped
2   cloves garlic, minced
    zest of 1 orange
⅓   cup finely chopped fresh parsley
    salt and pepper, to taste
    cayenne pepper, to taste
      (optional)
1   egg white, beaten
⅓   cup poppy seeds
⅓   cup sesame seeds
⅓   cup caraway seeds

Preparation

1. Mix flour with yeast and when well combined, add salt. Stir into the flour mixture 1 cup of warm water and the oil. Keep adding water as needed until dough is manageable. Beat about 6 minutes in stand mixer or knead by hand for at least 10 minutes.
2. Let dough rest 10 minutes, covered. Knead again and let stand another 15 minutes.
3. Divide the dough into three pieces. Cover a piece of dough with a sheet of plastic wrap and roll out dough as thin as possible. You can also use a pasta machine for this purpose. When finished, the dough should look like paper.
4. Preheat oven to 425°F.
5. Mix the onion, garlic, zest, and parsley. Season with salt and pepper; add cayenne pepper if desired. Set aside.
6. Line baking sheets (you will need four) with parchment paper.
7. Brush dough with egg white and sprinkle flatbread with onion mixture and seeds. Cut into squares, rectangles, or triangles and bake until golden, about 8 to 10 minutes.

Difficulty

Easy to Intermediate

Preparation

2 hours

Portion

60 pieces

SESAME RINGS

These little rings, sprinkled with sesame, are delicious with a cup of tea.

Preparation

1. Add sugar to water and stir. Dissolve yeast in water. Leave, covered, 7 minutes.
2. Combine the flour, semolina flour, yeast mixture, milk, olive oil and salt until a sticky dough forms. Knead 3 minutes. Cover and let rise 30 minutes.
3. Add more flour if needed to make the dough workable. Knead well to combine. Continue kneading about 6 minutes. Grease a bowl with oil, place dough in bowl, and let dough rise for 2 hours.
4. Preheat oven to 375°F.
5. Punch down dough. Cut dough into 20 pieces of approximately 2 inches. Form into long rolls, then twist ends together to form rings. Brush rings with egg and dip in the seeds. Let stand 15 minutes.
6. Bake for 20 minutes until rings begin to brown.

Ingredients

- 1 teaspoon sugar
- ⅔ cup water
- 1 tablespoon granulated dry yeast
- 2¼ cups flour (approximately)
- ½ cup semolina flour
- 1 cup milk
- 2 tablespoons olive oil
- ½ teaspoon salt
- 1 egg, beaten
- ¾ cup sesame seeds

Difficulty

Intermediate

Preparation

4 hours

Portion

20 rings

POPPY SEED AND ONION SPIRALS

These delicious rolls offer maximum reward for a little effort. Savory onion and poppy seeds are swirled inside a simple bread dough for a tasty treat.

Preparation

1. In a bowl, stir together the flour with the salt and sugar. Add the instant yeast.
2. In a separate bowl, mix together the 3 eggs, water, and oil. Add to the flour mixture and knead approximately 8 minutes or until the dough is smooth.
3. Place dough in a greased bowl, cover with plastic wrap, and let rise until doubled in size, about 2 to 3 hours.
4. Make the filling: While the dough is rising, cook the minced onion in a pan with oil until caramelized—it will take 30 to 40 minutes to get the onions well caramelized. Add salt and pepper to taste.
5. On a lightly floured surface, roll the dough into a thin rectangle, approximately 28 by 36 inches. Brush the dough with oil and spread with the caramelized onions. Sprinkle the surface with the poppy seeds.
6. Beginning with the long edge of the rectangle, roll the dough tightly. Press your fingers along the seam of the roll to seal.
7. With a sharp knife, cut the roll into 1-inch slices and place on a baking sheet or in a cupcake tin that has been greased and floured. Brush with beaten egg and let rise 30 minutes.
8. While the dough is rising, preheat oven to 375°F.
9. Bake spirals until golden, approximately 20 minutes. Let cool on a wire rack.

Ingredients

5 cups flour, plus extra for flouring surface
1 teaspoon salt
⅔ cup sugar
1½ tablespoons instant yeast
3 large eggs
¾ cup warm water (approximately)
¼ cup vegetable oil
1 egg, beaten
For the filling:
3 onions, finely minced
   vegetable oil, for cooking onions and brushing dough
   salt and pepper, to taste
⅓ cup poppy seeds

Difficulty

Easy to Intermediate

Preparation

4 hours

Portion

36 spirals

BUNS WITH CARAWAY

Caraway seeds give these simple buns a truly special flavor.

Ingredients

5	cups flour, plus extra
1	tablespoon salt
1½	tablespoons instant yeast
1	tablespoons caraway seeds
1	cup warm water, plus more as needed
¼	cup olive oil

Preparation

1. Mix flour and salt well. Add yeast. Mix in seeds.
2. Mix 1 cup water and the oil together and add to the flour mixture.
3. Knead, adding more water as needed until a sticky dough forms. Cover and let rise 2 hours.
4. Form dough into 2-inch rolls and cut a slit in the top. Dip in flour. Place on greased and floured baking sheet, 2 inches appart.
5. Let rise 30 minutes.
6. Preheat oven to 400°F.
7. Brush with water and immediately place in oven. Bake for 20 minutes, until they sound hollow.

Difficulty

Easy

Preparation

3 hours

Portion

24 rolls

ENGLISH MUFFINS

Homemade English muffins are a terrific treat. These particular ones make a truly special base for eggs Benedict!

Preparation

1. Heat milk and butter together over low heat until butter is melted. Remove from stove. Add yeast and water and let fluff.
2. In the bowl of a stand mixer, beat together the yeast mixture with the remaining ingredients (except cornmeal), adding the baking soda last. Beat 2 minutes.
3. Cover the dough well and let rest until doubled in size, 2 to 3 hours. The dough will be very sticky.
4. Preheat oven to 375°F.
5. Roll out the dough to about a 1-inch thickness, and cut in 3-to 3½-inch circles. Dip muffins in cornmeal. Flatten and place on a baking sheet lined with parchment paper.
6. Bake 20 minutes. Cool on wire rack.

Ingredients

1⅔	cups milk
2½	tablespoons butter
1	tablespoon active dry yeast
⅓	cup warm water
1	tablespoon sugar
1	large egg
2	teaspoons salt
2	teaspoons vinegar
5	cups flour
½	teaspoon baking soda
	cornmeal, for dusting

Difficulty

Easy

Preparation

3 to 4 hours

Portion

20 muffins

PITA BREAD

Pita is served at nearly every Middle Eastern meal and has become a favorite around the world. Fill the pockets with healthy sandwich ingredients or cut the bread into triangles for dipping.

Preparation

1. Stir together the flour with the salt and sugar. Mix well and add the yeast.
2. Whisking constantly, add warm water to form a sticky dough. Knead the dough in the bowl of a stand mixer for at least 5 minutes; if you are kneading by hand, it will likely take 10 to 15 minutes. This step is very important!
3. Once the dough is smooth and elastic, cut it into 8 to 10 equal pieces.
4. Roll the dough pieces into balls about an inch or so wide. Sprinkle flour lightly on a clean table and place the dough on the floured surface with the smooth side up and seam side down.
5. Cover with plastic wrap or a bread cloth and let stand about 15 minutes.
6. In the order they were made, flatten each of the balls on a floured surface and stretch them to about a 7-inch round. You can use a rolling pin to do this if you like. Be sure to dust off excess flour.
7. Place the breads by threes in a hot, nonstick pan, adjusting the heat as the pita breads are cooking. Let the breads puff up, gently patting with a paper towel while in the pan and turning them with a spatula. When they are puffed and golden, after about 3 or 4 minutes, remove from heat and place in a plastic bag immediately. Seal to keep them fresh.
   Note: Wipe the pan lightly with a paper towel before cooking each batch. Loose flour left in the pan will burn and will give the pitas cooked later a burnt taste if it is not removed.
   You can also bake the pitas in the oven at 375°F for about 10 to 12 minutes.

Ingredients

3½	cups flour, plus extra
1½	teaspoons salt
1	teaspoon sugar
1	tablespoon instant yeast
1–1½	cups warm water

Difficulty

Easy to Intermediate

Preparation

1 hour

Portion

8 to 10 pita breads

CRISPY BREADSTICKS

These tasty breadsticks are known as grissini in Italy—crisp and flavorful, they're the perfect starter for a meal or a wonderful addition to a cocktail menu. Form them in varying lengths to add interest to a basket of bread.

Ingredients

3–3¼	cups flour
½	teaspoon white pepper
1	teaspoon salt
1	teaspoon sugar
1	teaspoon instant yeast
¼	cup finely chopped fresh herbs (sage, rosemary, oregano, basil)
2	teaspoons extra-virgin olive oil
1	cup water
1	egg, beaten
	sesame, caraway, and poppy seeds, for sprinkling

Preparation

1. Mix dry ingredients and herbs and form a mound with a well in the center.
2. In a separate bowl, combine the 2 tablespoons olive oil and water. Add oil and water mixture to the well, mixing with a fork until dough is manageable. Knead for a few minutes.
3. Place the dough in a greased bowl, cover it tightly with plastic wrap, and put it in the refrigerator. Let rest overnight or at least 2 hours.
4. Preheat oven to 350°F.
5. Cut dough into approximately 30 or 40 pieces and form long, thin breadsticks by rolling between your hands and a clean, lightly floured surface. Place them ½ inch apart on greased and floured baking sheets.
6. Brush breadsticks with beaten egg and sprinkle with seeds. Bake until golden, about 25 to 30 minutes, rotating halfway through baking. Cool on a wire rack.

Difficulty

Intermediate

Preparation

3 to 4 hours

Portion

30 to 40 breadsticks

SODA BREADSTICKS

It is important to use mineral water in this recipe, because it makes the breadsticks crisper. I like to form these breadsticks in different lengths, then arrange them in a vase for the table, where they are both appetizer and decoration!

Preparation

1. Mix together the flour, sugar, and salt. Stir in yeast and mineral water, adding more mineral water as needed to form a very soft dough.
2. Beat 2 minutes in a stand mixer and let the dough rest for 20 minutes. Add oil and beat for 5 to 6 minutes until the dough is elastic. Cover and let double in size, 2 to 3 hours.
3. Cut the dough into three pieces. Roll out each piece of dough to a thin rectangle ¼ inch thick and 24 by 30 inches. Cut long strips of dough, roll them into breadstick shapes, and give each a few twists.
4. Preheat oven to 375°F.
5. Place breadsticks ½ inch apart on a baking sheet lined with parchment paper and let rise about 15 minutes.
6. Brush with egg white and sprinkle with seeds, to taste.
7. Sprinkle with coarse salt, if desired.
8. Bake until golden, 10 to 15 minutes. Cool on a wire rack.

Ingredients

6 cups flour
1 tablespoon sugar
1 tablespoon salt
1 tablespoon instant yeast
2 cups mineral water, approximately, at room temperature
⅓ cup vegetable oil
1 egg white, beaten
sesame or poppy seeds, for sprinkling
coarse salt, for sprinkling (optional)

Difficulty

Intermediate

Preparation

3 to 4 hours

Portion

150 breadsticks

ZUCCHINI-FILLED RING

Stuffed breads are among my favorites things. They're perfect all alone or paired with good coffee. And they also look beautiful—you can sprinkle this bread with black sesame seeds to make the presentation even more dramatic!

Preparation

1. To make the dough: add sugar to warm milk and stir. Dissolve yeast in milk for 5 minutes.
2. Add remaining ingredients (except melted butter), and knead until dough forms. Place in a bowl, cover with plastic wrap, and let double in size, 2 hours.
3. While dough is rising, make filling: cook in olive oil over low heat the peppers, parsley, and chives, adding broth and seasoning with salt and pepper. Add zucchini, mushrooms, and corn. Allow to dry completely. Adjust seasoning if needed. Allow to cool and mix with cheese.
4. Preheat oven to 375°F.
5. Roll out dough into a long rectangle 12 by 18 inches, and brush with half of the melted butter. Spread the filling across the rectangle, then roll tightly. Seal the seam of the dough and place in ring- shaped, greased and floured pan.
6. Let rise 15 minutes, then bake for 25 minutes.

Ingredients

1	teaspoon sugar
¾	cup warm milk
1	teaspoon dry yeast
½	teaspoon salt
2½	cups flour
¼	cup melted butter
1	egg yolk

For the filling:

1	tablespoon olive oil
1	sweet pepper, finely chopped
2	tablespoons finely chopped fresh parsley
⅓	cup finely chopped chives
1	tablespoon vegetable broth salt and pepper, to taste
2	zucchini, halved lengthwise, cored, and finely chopped
1	cup sliced mushrooms
2	cups sweet corn, without juice
2	cups grated gouda
¼	cup butter

Difficulty

Intermediate

Preparation

4 hours

Portion

1 loaf or ring

FAVORITE SWEET YEAST BREADS

Cinnamon Raisin Bread • Sweet Crescent Rolls • Cinnamon Twists • Rich Cinnamon Rolls • Sweet Camp Bread • Dulce de Leche Croissants • Spanish Sweet Bread • New Orleans Beignets • Babka Filled with Poppy Seeds, Nuts and Raisins • Rum Balls • Sweet Rolls Filled with Dulce de Leche and Figs • Chocolate Chip Braids • Lemon–Rosemary Brioches • Orange-Filled Rolls • Brioches • Spiced Fruit Bread • Sweet Roll Filled with Figs

CINNAMON RAISIN BREAD

Cinnamon and raisins just go together, right? This bread is certain to become a favorite!

Ingredients

1	cup warm milk
1⅓	cups warm water
1	egg, beaten
¼	cup butter, melted
6½	cups flour
1	tablespoon pure cocoa
1	tablespoon instant yeast
1	teaspoon salt
½	cup sugar
1¼	cups raisins, chopped
2	egg yolks
4	tablespoons milk
	For the filling:
2	cups brown sugar
3	tablespoons cinnamon

Preparation

1. Combine the warm milk, water, beaten egg, and butter. Set aside.
2. In a stand mixer, combine the flour, cocoa, yeast, salt, and sugar. Pour the liquid into the flour mixture and beat 10 minutes. Add the raisins and mix a few more minutes.
3. Place the dough in a greased bowl, cover, and let rest until doubled in size, 2 to 3 hours.
4. Divide the dough into three pieces. Stretch each piece into a rectangle about 9 by 12 inches.
5. Mix together the brown sugar and cinnamon for the filling. Sprinkle it over the dough. Roll each rectangle tightly and place each in a loaf pan that has been greased and floured.
6. Preheat oven to 375°F.
7. Let bread stand 20 minutes.
8. Mix egg yolks and the 4 tablespoons milk. Brush tops of breads with egg wash and bake until golden, about 25 to 30 minutes.

Difficulty

Easy

Preparation

4–5 hours

Portion

3 loaves

SWEET CRESCENT ROLLS

Called medialunas in Argentina, these sweet crescent rolls are reminiscent of French crois-
sants, but are smaller and brushed with a sweet glaze. I learned to make these rolls in
Argentina, where they are a breakfast staple.

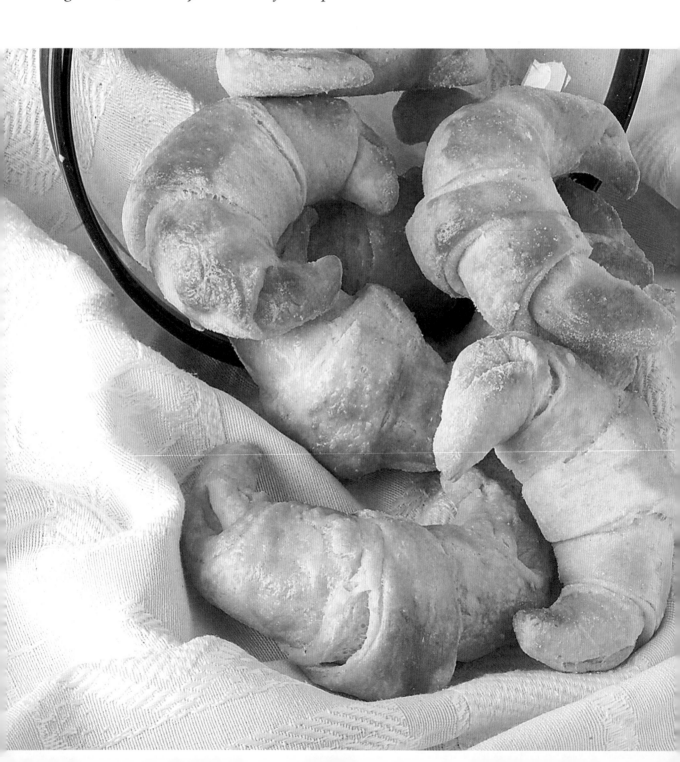

Preparation

1. Stir together the flour, sugar, salt, and yeast. Add lemon zest and stir.
2. In a separate bowl, mix milk, eggs, and yolks, then stir the wet ingredients into the flour mixture. Beat for about 5 to 6 minutes in a stand mixer. Add butter and beat 3 minutes.
3. Cover and rest the dough 15 minutes.
4. Place the dough on a lightly floured surface, then stretch with your fingers or roll with a rolling pin into a 16-by-16 inch square.
5. Make the filling: Beat together the 1½ cups margarine and 1½ cups flour for the filling, forming a paste.
6. Place the filling in the center of the dough square and fold the dough over the filling so that the bottom and top edges of the square meet, sealing in the filling. Pinch together the edges of the dough all around to secure the filling inside.
7. On a floured surface, stretch or roll the dough into a rectangle of about 12 by 16 inches. Fold the dough in thirds, as you would a letter that was going into an envelope. Rest the dough 30 minutes.
8. Again, roll the dough to a 12-by-16 inch rectangle, then fold in thirds and rest for 30 minutes. Repeat this process once more, resting the dough again. Ideally, let the dough sit overnight in the refrigerator before using, and roll and fold it a fourth time once it comes out of the refrigerator.
9. Stretch or roll out the dough to a thickness of about ⅛ inch, forming a large square. Cut the dough into three equal parts; each part will be a rectangle. Cut about 12 triangles from each of the three pieces of dough. Roll each triangle from the wide end toward the pointed end, then curve to make a half-moon shape.
10. Place the crescents on baking sheets (you will need three) that have been greased and floured.
11. Cover and let the dough rest 1 hour. While dough is resting, preheat oven to 425°F.
12. Bake crescents until they begin to brown, approximately 15 to 20 minutes.
13. Make the glaze: Boil water with sugar to form a syrup, about 5 minutes. Set aside to cool.
14. Once the crescents have cooled, use a pastry brush to glaze each crescent.

Ingredients

6½	cups flour
¾	cup sugar
1	teaspoon salt
1½	tablespoons instant yeast
	zest of 1 lemon
1½	cups milk
3	eggs
2	egg yolks
½	cup butter (1 stick) at room temperature
1	teaspoon vanilla

For the filling:

1½	cups butter (3 sticks) at room temperature
1½	cups flour

For the glaze:

1	cup water
1	cup sugar

Difficulty

Intermediate

Preparation

5 hours

Portion

36 crescents

CINNAMON TWISTS

Delightfully sweetened with brown sugar and cinnamon, these twists are perfect served for Sunday brunch.

Preparation

1. Mix 6 cups flour and yeast and stir well. Add salt, baking soda, and sugar.
2. In a separate bowl, lightly beat the eggs with the 2 cups warm milk. Add ½ cup butter and mix with flour. The dough should be sticky. If you need more liquid, add additional warm milk.
3. Cover the dough and let rise, 3 to 4 hours.
4. Punch down dough and knead about 5 minutes in mixer or 10 minutes by hand, using extra flour if needed. Divide dough into three portions.
5. Mix together brown sugar and cinnamon for filling.
6. Roll one portion of the dough into a rectangular shape about 12 by 14 inches and spread with softened butter. Sprinkle a third of the brown sugar mixed with cinnamon over the dough and fold the dough in half. Repeat with the other two portions of dough.
7. Cut each portion of dough across the width into 1-inch strips and twist one or two turns (see photo). Place on baking sheets lined with parchment paper, leaving at least 1 inch between each twist.
8. Preheat oven to 375°F.
9. Let twists rise 20 minutes. Bake until golden, about 15 to 20 minutes.
10. To make icing: stir together melted butter and powdered sugar, and add milk, adding more milk as needed to make a spreadable glaze. When twists come out of the oven, brush with glaze. Allow to dry.

Ingredients

6	cups flour, plus extra if needed
2	teaspoons instant yeast
1	teaspoon salt
½	teaspoon baking soda
⅓	cup sugar
2	eggs
2	cups milk (or buttermilk), warmed, plus more if needed
½	cup butter (1 stick), softened

For filling:

1½	cups brown sugar
3	tablespoons ground cinnamon
¾	cup butter, softened

For icing (optional):

1	ounce (¼ stick) butter, melted
1½	cups powdered sugar, sifted
1	cup warm milk, approximately

Difficulty

Intermediate

Preparation

5 hours

Portion

36 to 40 twists

RICH CINNAMON ROLLS

This is a recipe I come back to again and again. The rolls are so sweet and delicious, you will thank me—and your family will thank you!

Preparation

1. Line two 9- or 10-inch round baking pans with parchment paper.
2. Mix together flour, yeast, sugar, and salt.
3. In a separate bowl, combine the milk, eggs, and oil. Combine the wet and dry mixtures and stir until a very sticky dough forms. If you need more milk, add it. Beat about 7 minutes in a stand mixer, or 15 minutes if you are mixing by hand.
4. Cover dough and let rise for at least 3 hours.
5. Make the filling: melt two sticks of butter. Combine the heavy cream with 2 cups brown sugar and the melted butter. Divide this mixture into the bottom of the two pans. Set aside.
6. Melt remaining stick of butter.
7. After the dough has risen, divide it into two parts. Using a rolling pin, roll out each piece of dough to a rectangle of about 15 by 18 inches.
8. Combine the remaining 1 cup brown sugar with the nuts, raisins, and cinnamon.
9. Brush each rectangle of dough with half of the melted butter. Spread half the raisin and nut mixture on each. Roll one rectangle of dough tightly. Do the same with the other half.
10. Cut each roll into 18 equal slices (about 1 inch each).
11. Place each piece in the cream mixture in the pans, turning once or twice so that both sides are coated with the mixture.
12. Preheat oven to 375°F.
13. Let the rolls rise 20 minutes. Bake for 25 to 30 minutes. Carefully invert onto a platter while warm.

Ingredients

7	cups flour
2	tablespoons instant yeast
¾	cup sugar
1	teaspoon salt
1¾–2	to 2 cups warm milk
3	eggs
⅓	cup vegetable oil

For the filling:

3	cups heavy cream
3	cups brown sugar
1½	cups (3 sticks) butter
1	cup coarsely chopped walnuts
1	cup raisins
½	cup ground cinnamon

Difficulty

Intermediate

Preparation

4 hours

Portion

36 rolls

SWEET CAMP BREAD

These yeast rolls are made with a little sugar and glazed with marmalade for a sweet twist on traditional camp bread.

Preparation

1. Mix the butter and shortening in a bowl, with ⅔ cup hot water to melt. Add 2 eggs and combine.
2. Mix the flour with raisins (if using), sugar, salt, and yeast. Add wet ingredients to the flour mixture to form a sticky dough. If you need more liquid, add it now. Beat 5 minutes.
3. Place dough in a greased bowl, cover with plastic wrap, and let rise until it doubles in size, approximately 3 hours.
4. Preheat oven to 375°F.
5. Cut or pinch off dough into 20 pieces. Form thick ropes of about 10 inches in length and wrap in spirals (see photo). Place in a greased and floured pan about 1 inch apart. Cover the pan and let rise 20 minutes.
6. Beat the egg with a pinch of salt and brush the tops of the breads. Bake until golden, about 15 minutes.
7. Mix the marmalade with 3 tablespoons water and heat until melted. While breads are still warm, brush tops with jam. Cool on wire rack.

Ingredients

¼	cup (½ stick) butter
2	tablespoons shortening
⅔	cup hot water, or more as necessary
2	eggs
4½	cups flour
½	cup raisins (optional)
½	cup sugar
1	teaspoon salt
1½	tablespoons instant yeast
1	egg, beaten
	pinch of salt
3	tablespoons orange marmalade
3	tablespoons water

Difficulty

Easy to Intermediate

Preparation

4 hours

Portion

20 to 24 rolls

DULCE DE LECHE CROISSANTS

From the first bite, you'll love these buttery croissants, which are rich with the caramel flavor of dulce de leche. Be careful, though, the filling can be hot!

Preparation

1. Mix together flour, yeast, sugar, and salt.
2. In a saucepan, mix heavy cream and water and heat until just warm. Take off heat and stir in shortening and 2 eggs.
3. Mix wet ingredients with flour mixture until a compact and manageable dough forms. If you need more flour to make the dough workable, add it. Beat about 7 minutes in a stand mixer. Place dough in a greased bowl, cover, and let rise at least 2 hours.
4. Mix the dulce de leche with the cornstarch. Set aside.
5. Roll the dough into a rectangle about 26 by 34 inches and spread half the butter over the dough. Bring the edges of the rectangle to the center of the dough, then fold in half, forming a book. Refrigerate at least 20 minutes.
6. Roll dough out again to a rectangle about 24 to 36 inches, and brush with the other half of the butter. Fold rectangle by thirds, as if you were folding a letter into an envelope, and refrigerate 20 minutes.
7. Preheat oven to 375°F.
8. Roll the dough to a thickness of about ⅛ inch. Cut into strips, then cut strips on the diagonal into triangles (see photo). Place a small dab of the dulce de leche in the center of each triangle. Fold one triangle point over the filling and toward the opposite long edge, tucking the point under the edge of the dough; curve the ends to form a croissant shape (see photo).
9. Place croissants on greased and floured baking sheets and let rise 20 minutes.
10. Brush with beaten egg and bake 20 to 25 minutes.
11. Cool on wire rack and sprinkle with powdered sugar, if desired.
    *Note: Dulce de leche is available in some groceries or online, or make your own using the recipe in the appendix.

Ingredients

5 cups flour, plus extra as needed
2 tablespoons instant yeast
⅓ cup sugar
1 teaspoon salt
½ cup heavy cream
¾ cup warm water
⅓ cup melted shortening
2 eggs
1¾ cups dulce de leche*
2 teaspoons cornstarch
½ cup (1 stick) butter, softened
1 egg, beaten
½ cup powdered sugar, sifted (optional)

Difficulty

Intermediate

Preparation

4 hours

Portion

30 croissants

SPANISH SWEET BREAD

Spread with marmalade, this sweet bread makes a marvelous breakfast. It's also great as a late-afternoon pick-me-up meal, which the Spanish call la merienda.

Ingredients

For the topping:
- 5 tablespoons toasted almonds
- 3 tablespoons plus 2 teaspoons sugar
- 1 egg white, beaten (or more, as needed)

For the dough:
- 2 cups bread flour
- 5 teaspoons instant yeast
- 1½ ounces (⅜ stick) butter
- 3 tablespoons sugar
- 1 teaspoon salt
- 5 tablespoons water
- 2 teaspoons powdered milk
- 1 egg
- 1 tablespoon lemon zest
- 1 tablespoon vanilla

Preparation

1. Make the topping: Put the almonds and the sugar into a food processor and mix until fine. Add enough egg white to form a spreadable paste. Reserve any leftover egg white to brush bread.
2. Make the dough: Mix the flour and yeast together, and form a mound with a well.
3. Mix other dough ingredients (except for topping) into the flour and knead for 10 minutes, until the dough is very thin. Cover tightly and let stand 30 minutes in a warm area.
4. Divide the dough in half and make two balls. Place on a greased and floured baking sheet and let rise for 20 minutes, punch down, and let rise again until doubled in size, 2 to 3 hours.
5. Preheat oven to 350°F.
6. Brush the surface of the bread with egg white and spread with the almond paste.
7. Bake about 40 to 45 minutes.

Difficulty

Easy

Preparation

3 to 4 hours

Portion

2 loaves

104

NEW ORLEANS BEIGNETS

Eat these sweet Crescent City treats hot, ideally with a steaming cup of robust coffee.

Preparation

1. Mix the flour with the yeast. Add salt, sugar, nutmeg, cinnamon, and orange zest.
2. Add the warm milk and cream, incorporating into the flour mixture. Mix in eggs and vanilla. Beat 8 minutes in a stand mixer. Finally, incorporate butter. Beat another minute.
3. Place dough in a bowl, cover with plastic wrap, and refrigerate 3 hours.
4. Roll dough out into a 9-by-12-inch rectangle. Cut the dough into rectangles or squares approximately 1½ by 2 inches. Cover dough and chill again for about 15 minutes.
5. Stretch each dough square a little with your hands, then deep-fry in hot oil until golden, turning with a slotted spoon. Cook until the beignets are puffed, about 3 to 5 minutes.
6. Place immediately on paper towels to absorb excess oil.
7. Sift powdered sugar over the warm beignets.

Ingredients

3½	cups flour
1	tablespoon instant yeast
½	teaspoon salt
2	tablespoons sugar
½	teaspoon nutmeg
1	teaspoon cinnamon
1	tablespoon orange zest
½	cup warm milk, approximately
⅓	cup heavy cream
2	eggs
1	tablespoon vanilla
3	ounces (¾ stick) butter, diced and at room temperature
	vegetable oil, for frying
	powdered sugar, for sprinkling

Difficulty

Intermediate

Preparation

4 hours

Portion

36 beignets

BABKA FILLED WITH POPPY SEEDS, NUTS, AND RAISINS

This wonderful, old-fashioned dessert bread is filled with walnuts, poppy seeds, dried fruits, and spices, all traditional ingredients in Eastern European baking.

Preparation

1. Mix flour, sugar, salt, and yeast well.
2. In a separate bowl, mix together 2 eggs with the water and butter. Add wet ingredients to flour, beating at medium speed for at least 8 minutes.
3. Place the dough in a greased bowl and let rise 2 hours or until doubled in size.
4. Melt the marmalade and, once it's hot, stir in poppy seeds. Mix with the remaining filling ingredients and set aside.
5. Preheat oven to 325°F, then grease a baking sheet with butter.
6. Roll the dough into a long, narrow rectangle, about 12 by 20 inches. Brush with beaten egg, place the filling in the center, and roll dough tightly. Pinch seam to close. Form a into a circle and place on baking sheet or in a round cake pan, making sure that the seam side is facing down.
7. Brush top with melted butter and bake about 40 minutes, or until babka begins to brown. Cool on wire rack.
8. For the glaze: Mix the milk with sugar and add the zest. Drizzle over babka.
   *For more spirals inside of your Babka, after you place the filling, fold a second time. Roll tightly.

Ingredients

- 4 cups flour, plus extra
- ½ cup sugar
- 1 teaspoon salt
- 1 tablespoon instant yeast
- 2 large eggs
- 1 cup warm water
- ¾ cup butter, melted and cooled
- 1 egg, beaten

For the filling:
- ⅓ cup orange marmalade
- 1⅓ cup poppy seeds
- ⅔ cup brown sugar
- 2 tablespoons ground cinnamon
- 1 tablespoon grated orange peel
- ½ cup raisins
- ½ cup chopped toasted walnuts
- ¼ cup (½ stick) butter, melted and cooled
- 1 cup bread crumbs
- 1 egg

For the glaze:
- 2 tablespoons milk
- 3–4 cups powdered sugar
- 2 tablespoons orange zest

Difficulty

Intermediate

Preparation

4 hours

Portion

1 babka

RUM BALLS

My friend Herlan shared this recipe with me—it's divine, both to make and to eat! These rum balls are yeast-risen and rolled in cinnamon and nuts, then baked together to make a delicious pull-apart bread.

Ingredients

For the dough starter:
3 tablespoons instant yeast
½ cup milk
1 tablespoon sugar
1 tablespoon flour
For the dough:
1 teaspoon salt
½ cup sugar
2 eggs
1 tablespoon lemon zest
1 tablespoon orange zest
1 tablespoon vanilla
¼ cup rum
4 cups flour
½ cup (1 stick) butter, softened
For the topping:
1 cup sugar
2 cups finely chopped walnuts
2 tablespoons ground cinnamon
5 ounces melted butter

Preparation

1. Make the dough starter: combine all the ingredients for the dough starter and allow to sit for 10 minutes.
2. Grease and flour a large ring pan.
3. Combine 1 teaspoon salt, ½ cup sugar, 2 eggs, the lemon and orange zest, vanilla, and rum with the dough starter. Add flour.
4. Knead well. You must knead hard, as this is a dense dough. Let stand, covered, 30 minutes
5. Add butter and knead again, until butter is well integrated.
6. Make the topping: Combine sugar, walnuts, and cinnamon.
7. Form balls the size of a Ping-Pong ball.
8. Dip each ball in melted butter, then immediately roll in the
9. nut mixture and arrange close together in pan. Keep making the dough balls until there is no dough left
10. (there will be two or three layers of balls).
11. Cover tightly and let rise until dough doubles in size, about 3 hours.
12. Preheat oven to 350°F.
13. Bake the rum balls until they begin to brown, about 30 minutes.
14. Let cool for a few minutes on wire rack and turn out of the pan while still warm.

Difficulty

Intermediate

Preparation

5 hours

Portion

48 to 60 rum balls

SWEET ROLLS FILLED WITH DULCE DE LECHE AND FIGS

My grandchildren love this delectable sweet bread. The rolls can be baked and then frozen so they're always on hand. They should go directly from the freezer into the oven to reheat, without being defrosted first.

Preparation

1. Make the dough starter: Combine flour, yeast, and milk to form a compact dough. Oil the inside of a large food-safe plastic bag designed for cooking (such as for sous vide) and place dough inside. Press all air from the bag and seal or knot the top. Place bag in a large pan of warm water. Let rise 30 minutes.
2. Make the dough: Combine the 3 cups flour with yeast, sugar, salt, and zest. Stir well.
3. In a separate bowl, mix vanilla with egg yolks and milk. Pour egg and milk mixture into the flour mixture and stir well. Add the dough starter and knead. Finally, stir in the ½ cup butter and continue kneading until well incorporated.
4. Let dough rise until doubled in size, 2 to 3 hours.
5. Mix the figs with the dulce de leche and set aside.
6. Preheat oven to 350°F.
7. Cut dough into about 30 pieces, approximately 4 by 5 inches each, to form oval rolls. Place on baking sheets that have been greased and floured or lined with parchment paper. Let rise 20 minutes.
8. Brush rolls with melted butter and bake until golden, 20 to 25 minutes.
9. Cool on wire rack. Make a cut at the top of each roll with kitchen shears and fill with dulce de leche and fig filling. Sift powdered sugar over rolls before serving.
*Note: Dulce de Leche is available in some groceries or online, or make your own using the recipe in the appendix.

Ingredients

For the dough starter:
1¼ cups flour
1 tablespoon instant yeast
⅔ cup warm whole milk
For the dough:
3 cups flour
¼ cup sugar
2 teaspoons salt
1 tablespoon lemon zest
1 tablespoon vanilla
7 egg yolks
⅔ cup warm whole milk
½ cup (1 stick) butter, cut into small pieces and softened
¼ cup melted butter, for brushing rolls
sugar, for sprinkling
For the filling:
6 dried figs, diced
2 cups dulce de leche*

Difficulty

Intermediate

Preparation

6 hours

Portion

30 rolls

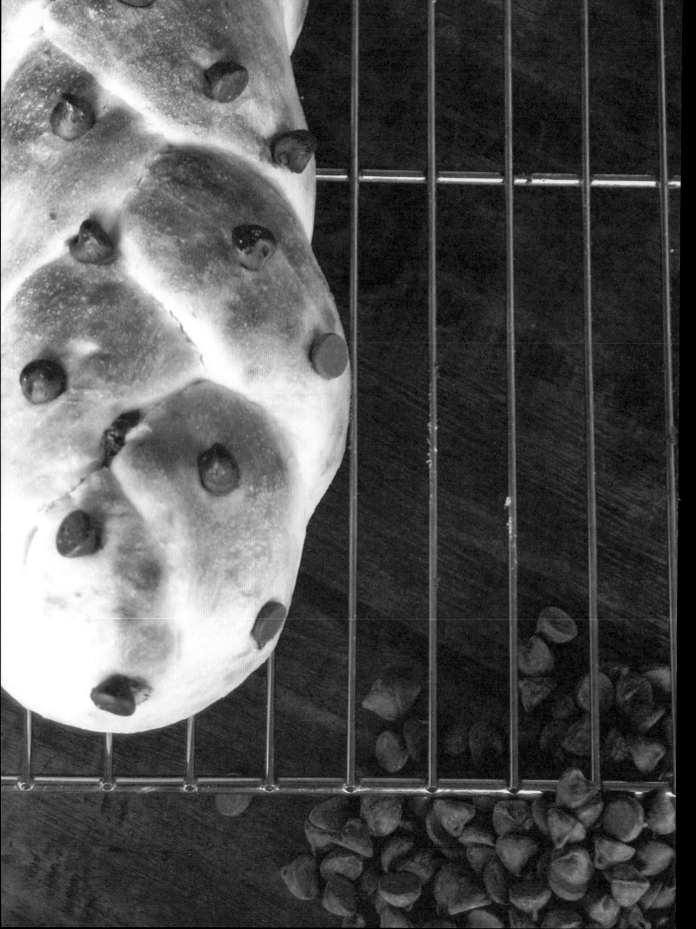

CHOCOLATE CHIP BRAIDS

A sweet treat for the ones you love. Plentiful chocolate chips will make your family worship you!

Preparation

1. Add the sugar to the boiling water and stir until sugar is fully dissolved. Add the butter and salt, and allow to melt completely. Add ¼ milk.
2. Beat the 4 eggs well by hand, and add them to the sugar and water mixture.
3. In a large bowl, put 8½ cups of the flour, reserving ½ cup.
4. Add the yeast to the flour, then add the sugar–water–egg mixture and stir. Fold in chocolate chips.
5. Knead the dough very well by hand, using reserved 1/2 cup of flour as needed, until smooth, about 10 minutes. Cover and let rise until dough doubles in size, about 2 hours.
6. Preheat oven to 350°F.
7. Make the braids: Cut dough into 12 balls. Stretch and form long, thick ropes, about 8 to 9 inches in length. Braid ropes into 4 braids and place on baking sheets that have been greased and floured or lined with parchment paper. Let stand 20 minutes.
8. Brush braids with egg yolk mixed with the 2 tablespoons of milk. Bake 20 minutes, or until golden.

Ingredients

1¼	cups sugar
1½	cups boiling water
¾	cup (1½ stick) butter
1	tablespoon salt
¼	cup milk
4	eggs
9	cups flour
2	tablespoons instant yeast
2	cups chocolate chips
1	egg yolk, beaten
2	tablespoons milk

Difficulty

Intermediate

Preparation

4 hours

Portion

4 braids

LEMON-ROSEMARY BRIOCHES

These spectacular lemon-kissed brioches make a wonderful accompaniment to afternoon tea.

Ingredients

- 4   cups flour, approximately
- 2   tablespoons instant yeast
- ¼   cup sugar
- 2   teaspoons salt
-     zest of 1 lemon
- 2   tablespoons chopped fresh rosemary
- 1¼ cups (2½ sticks) butter, softened
- 4   eggs
- 2   egg yolks
-     cup water, plus more as needed
- 1   egg, beaten

Preparation

1. Mix flour and yeast.
2. Add sugar, salt, zest, rosemary, and butter, and mix well.
3. Beat the 4 eggs with the 2 yolks and ⅓ cup water and add to mixture.
4. Continue kneading and adding water until dough is manageable but sticky.
5. Let dough rise overnight in the refrigerator, or at least 6 to 8 hours. Remove, knead, and let rise about 30 minutes at room temperature.
6. Preheat oven to 400°F.
7. Grease a brioche tin or cupcake pan. Form about 24 balls about 1½ inches wide and form the same number of balls about ½ inch wide.
8. Place the large dough balls in the pan.
9. Make a deep slit in the top of each brioche and press a small ball into each slit.
10. Brush with beaten egg and bake for 5 minutes. Lower the oven temperature to 375°F and continue baking until toothpick inserted comes out clean, about 15 minutes more.

Difficulty

Intermediate

Preparation

4 hours and 1 day

Portion

24 brioches

ORANGE-FILLED ROLLS

Perfect for breakfast, these sweet, glazed rolls have the sunshiny taste of fresh oranges!

Preparation

1. Make the filling: Melt butter and let cool. Add the orange zest, liqueur, and sugar and mix well. Add nuts to half the filling, leaving the other half plain.
2. Make the dough: Mix flour, sugar, and salt. Add yeast and stir well.
3. In a small saucepan, heat milk and butter over low heat until butter melts. Stir the milk and butter mixture and the egg into the flour. Knead for 10 minutes.
4. Let dough rise to double its size. Punch down dough and let rise another 15 minutes.
5. Roll or stretch the dough to form a rectangle of about 24 by 36 inches. Spread the dough with the of the filling containing nuts and roll dough tightly.
6. Preheat oven to 400°F.
7. Cut the roll into 2-inch pieces and place on a baking sheet lined with parchment paper. Let rise 20 minutes.
8. Bake until golden, 25 to 30 minutes.
9. Let cool a few minutes and drizzle rolls with the rest of the filling.

Ingredients

For the filling:
¼ cup (½ stick) butter
1 tablespoon orange zest
3 tablespoons orange liqueur
2 cups powdered sugar
½ cup finely chopped nuts (any type)
For the dough:
3½ cups flour, approximately
¼ cup sugar
1 teaspoon salt
1 tablespoon instant yeast
1 cup milk
¼ cup butter
1 egg

Difficulty

Easy

Preparation

4 hours

Portion

18 rolls

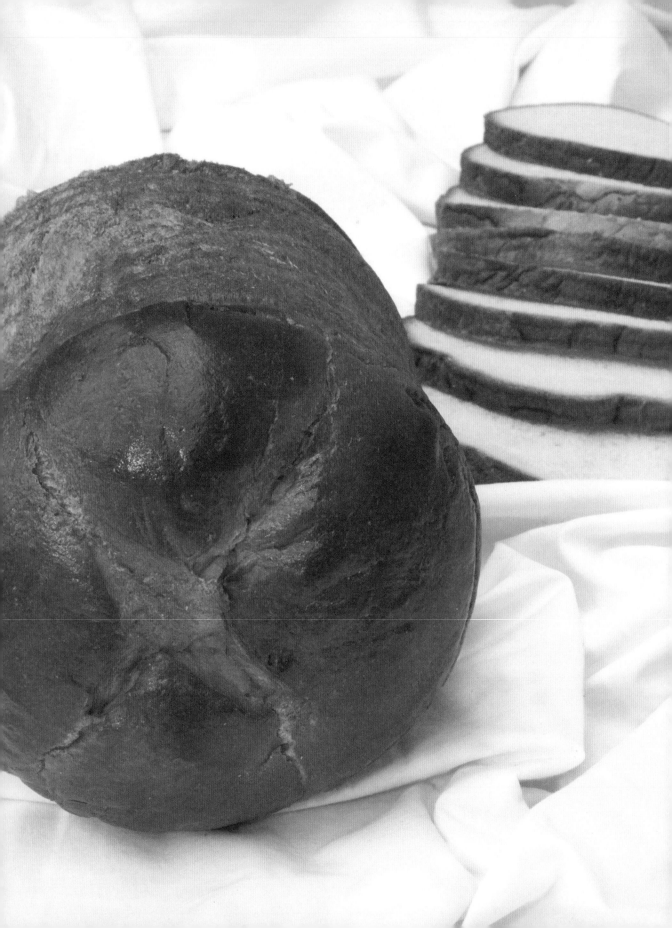

BRIOCHES

Plentiful eggs and butter in this rich, French bread give it a soft and tender crumb. A special pan will lend the bread its characteristic shape.

Preparation

1. Place the yeast in water with 1 teaspoon of the sugar and allow yeast to swell for 10 minutes. Add 1 cup of flour. Form a ball and let rest 30 minutes (this is the starter dough).
2. In a separate bowl, beat together the remaining flour, salt, sugar, and the 10 eggs.
3. Knead until a dough forms. Add the starter dough and continue kneading until dough is smooth.
4. Finally, incorporate the butter and knead hard for 3 minutes, until the dough pulls away from the bowl. The dough should be smooth and very elastic.
5. Cover dough and let rest until it doubles in size, 4 to 5 hours.
6. Punch down the dough and let it rest in the refrigerator overnight, for use the next day. After you take the dough from the refrigerator, punch it down again.
7. Take three-quarters of the dough and cut into 48 pieces, and roll them into balls the size of a large walnut. Take the remaining one-quarter of the dough and cut into 48 pieces about the size of a grape. Make a slit in the large balls and, with your thumb, widen the pocket in the center of each.
8. Place the smallest ball inside the slit.
9. Place in greased brioche pan or cupcake tin.
10. Allow 90 minutes to rise at room temperature.
11. Preheat oven to 400°F.
12. Brush brioches with beaten egg and bake about 12 minutes.

Ingredients

1½	tablespoons active dry yeast
1	cup warm water, approximately
⅔	cup sugar
8	cups flour
1	tablespoon salt
10	eggs
3½	cups butter (7 sticks), softened
1	egg, beaten

Difficulty

Intermediate

Preparation

8 hours and 1 day

Portion

48 brioches

115

SPICED FRUIT BREAD

Fragrant with cinnamon and citrus, this bread is truly spectacular. For Christmas, I like to shape the bread into a festive candy cane form.

Ingredients

1	cup chopped raisins
⅔	cup boiling water
2	tablespoons active dry yeast
¾	cup warm milk
1	tablespoon white sugar
⅓	cup brown sugar
¾	cup whole wheat flour
3–3½	cups white flour
⅓	brown sugar
2	teaspoons salt
1/8	teaspoon ground cloves
½	teaspoon fresh grated nutmeg
1½	teaspoons fresh ground ginger
1	teaspoon ground cinnamon
1	cup chopped crystallized ginger
½	cup chopped candied cherries
1	teaspoon grated lemon peel
1	teaspoon grated orange peel
3	ounces (¾ stick) butter, melted
2	eggs
1	egg yolk (reserve the white for use in topping)
	For the topping:
1	egg white
3	tablespoons powdered sugar, sifted

Preparation

1. Place the raisins in the boiling water and let them puff up. Reserve the liquid.
2. Place the yeast in warm milk with 1 tablespoon white sugar. Stir well and let yeast fluff until it forms a froth.
3. Combine flour with brown sugar, salt, spices, and the other ingredients. Beat well. If you need more liquid, add a bit of water. The dough will be very sticky. Beat 5 to 7 minutes on medium speed until the dough is smooth.
4. Let dough rest until doubled in size, about 2 to 3 hours.
5. Stretch or roll the dough into a rectangle of about 24 by 30 inches. Fold in half and place on baking sheet that has been greased and floured or lined with parchment
6. paper.
7. Let dough stand 20 minutes.
8. While dough is rising, preheat oven to 350°F.
9. Bake 18 minutes.
   While bread is baking, whisk the egg white with the pow-
10. dered sugar to form a soft meringue.
    Remove bread from oven and cover with meringue.
11. Bake for 5 more minutes.
    Cool on wire rack.

Difficulty

Easy

Preparation

4 hours

Portion

1 loaf

116

SWEET ROLL FILLED WITH FIGS

I make these sweet, fig-laden rolls at Christmastime and give them as special gifts to friends and family members, so this recipe makes a large quantity. I guarantee everyone will love them!

Preparation

1. Make the filling: Cook the figs over medium heat in ½ cup water mixed with sugar, zest, and cinnamon until soft, about 20 minutes.
2. Remove cinnamon sticks and skim off zest. Mash figs in their own syrup.
3. Mix milk with cornstarch and heat, stirring, until thick. Add the figs and let cool.
4. Make the dough: Place 7 cups flour in a large bowl or in the bowl of a stand mixer. Add the yeast and mix well.
5. Add salt and sugar and the water. Stir the mixture well with a wooden spoon, cover with plastic wrap, and allow to rise at least 1 hour.
6. In a separate bowl, mix together the eggs and oil and stir into the dough.
7. Slowly begin adding the remaining flour, until dough is manageable (you may not need entire amount). Knead about 10 minutes and let rise, covered, for 5 to 8 hours.
8. Punch down dough and divide into three equal parts
9. Roll one piece of the dough into a rectangle about 24 by 30 inches. Spread one-third of the filling over two-thirds of the rectangle.
10. Fold the dough in thirds, taking care to pinch seams on all sides so that they will not open during baking. Repeat steps 9 and 10 with the other two pieces of dough.
11. Place on greased and floured baking sheets.
12. Brush rolls with melted butter and cut a slit in the top with a sharp knife. Let rise 1 hour.
13. Preheat oven to 375°F while rolls are rising.
14. Bake 25 minutes, or until golden.
15. While still hot, sift powdered sugar over the rolls. Cool on wire rack.

Ingredients

For the filling:

24	dried figs
½	cup water
1	cup sugar, or to taste
	zest of 3 lemons (no white rind)
3	cinnamon sticks
1½	cups milk
3	tablespoons cornstarch

For the dough:

14	cups flour, approximately
2	tablespoons instant yeast
1	teaspoon salt
1½	cups sugar
3½	cups warm water
3	eggs
½	cup vegetable oil
1–2	ounces (¼–½ stick) melted butter
	powdered sugar, sifted, for sprinkling

Difficulty

Intermediate

Preparation

4 hours plus 8 hours

Portion

3 large rolls

MOUTHWATERING SAVORY QUICK BREADS

Beer Bread with Sun-Dried Tomatoes and Olives • Parmesan Biscuits • Biscuits • Skillet Cornbread • Garlic Bread with Black Olives • Brazilian Cheese Rolls • Rosemary Popovers • Colombian Cheese Buns • Bolivian Cassava Buns • Quick Rolls with Chives and Caraway

BEER BREAD WITH SUN-DRIED TOMATOES AND OLIVES

Strong in flavor, with a lovely dense texture, this is the perfect bread to pair with sausages or sardines. It's best eaten the same day it comes out of the oven.

Ingredients

- 3½ cups flour
- 1 teaspoon salt
- 1½ teaspoons baking soda
- 1 teaspoon baking powder
- 12 ounces (1½ cups) beer
- 1 egg, lightly beaten
- ½ cup sun-dried tomatoes packed in oil, chopped (reserve 2 tablespoons of the liquid)
- ⅓ cup pimento-stuffed olives

Preparation

1. Preheat oven to 350°F. Grease and flour two 5-by-9-inch loaf pans.
2. Mix together the flour, salt, baking soda, and baking powder. Add the beer, egg, sun-dried tomatoes, reserved liquid from the tomatoes, and olives.
3. Beat on medium speed 10 minutes and spread batter in pan.
4. Bake 40 minutes or until a toothpick inserted into the center of the bread comes out clean.

Difficulty

Easy

Preparation

1 hour

Portion

2 loaf

PARMESAN BISCUITS

These delightful biscuits are made rich with buttermilk and a healthy dose of Parmesan.

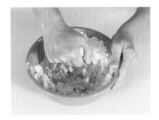 

Preparation

1. Preheat oven to 400°F.
2. Mix flour, baking powder, and salt. Dice the shortening and add to the flour mixture. Add the buttermilk and knead lightly, only 11 to 12 times.
3. Pat or roll the dough out to a rectangle of about 8 by 10 inches. Cut circles of about 2¼ inches and place on a baking sheet that has been greased and floured or lined with parchment paper.
4. Brush with the melted butter and sprinkle with Parmesan. Bake until golden, about 20 minutes.

Ingredients

2 cups flour
4 teaspoons baking powder
1 teaspoon salt
½ cup shortening
¾ cup buttermilk
1 ounce melted butter
3 tablespoons grated Parmesan

Difficulty

Easy to Intermediate

Preparation

1 hour

Portion

12 biscuits

BISCUITS

These soft, flaky biscuits are so rewarding to bake—they take almost no time to make and liven up any meal.

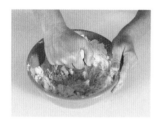 

Ingredients

2	cups flour
4	teaspoons baking powder
¼	teaspoon baking soda
¾	teaspoon salt
1	ounce (¼ stick) butter, cold
2	tablespoons shortening
1	cup cold buttermilk melted butter, for brushing dough

Preparation

1. Preheat oven to 375°F.
2. Combine flour, baking powder, baking soda, and salt.
3. Using a pastry blender or two butter knives, cut butter and shortening into dry ingredients until it forms a consistency like cornmeal.
4. Add buttermilk and combine without kneading (you do not want to melt the fat). It will form a sticky dough.
5. Place dough on a floured board, and roll or pat to a thickness of ⅓ inch. Cut in circles, using a 2-inch cookie cutter or the rim of a glass.
6. Place biscuits ½ inch apart on a baking sheet that has been greased and floured or lined with parchment paper. Brush with melted butter and bake until golden, 15 to 20 minutes.

Difficulty
Easy

Preparation
1 hour

Portion
18 biscuits

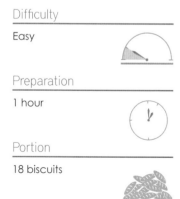

SKILLET CORNBREAD

I learned to make this bread in New Orleans—it's fun to bake right in the skillet, and the recipe is so simple and good! A black cast-iron skillet is a necessity.

Preparation

1. Preheat oven to 425°F. Coat the inside of a cast-iron skillet with vegetable oil and heat in the oven for about 5 minutes. Lower temperature to 375°F.
2. Mix the dry ingredients in a bowl. Set aside.
3. In a separate bowl, beat eggs, butter, and buttermilk together. Mix wet ingredients with dry ingredients just to incorporate.
4. Spoon batter into the skillet and bake at 375°F about 35 to 40 minutes. Cool in the skillet on a wire rack before slicing.

Ingredients

2–3	tablespoons vegetable oil
2	cups coarse cornmeal
2	cups flour
3	teaspoons baking powder
1	teaspoon baking soda
1	teaspoon salt
⅓	cup sugar
4	large eggs
½	cup (1 stick) butter, melted
2½	cups buttermilk

Difficulty

Easy

Preparation

1 hour

Portion

1 round bread

GARLIC BREAD WITH BLACK OLIVES

Peppery arugula and imported ham, together with a cold beer, are perfect pairings for this robust bread flavored with black olives and plenty of garlic.

Ingredients

3	cups flour
1½	tablespoons baking powder
2	eggs
⅓	cup olive oil
⅓	cup sour cream
1	teaspoon salt
2	tablespoons sugar
⅓	cup warm water, approximately
5	cloves garlic, minced
⅔	cup sliced black olives

Preparation

1. Grease and flour a loaf pan. Preheat oven to 375°F.
2. Mix flour with baking powder and set aside.
3. Beat eggs, oil, sour cream, salt, and sugar together. Stir flour mixture into egg and sour cream mixture. Add ⅓ cup warm water, and mix well. Add more water as needed to make a dough that is soft and manageable. Beat for 3 to 4 minutes. Add garlic and olives and stir 1 minute more.
4. Place dough in loaf pan that has been greased and floured, and bake until golden brown, about 30 minutes.

Difficulty

Easy

Preparation

1 hour

Portion

1 loaf

BRAZILIAN CHEESE ROLLS

Cassava flour is widely used throughout Central and South America, and is catching on in the United States as well. Cassava flour is also called tapioca flour, but note that tapioca starch is different—it is processed to extract the maximum amount of starch of the cassava, and does not contain the proteins and fiber of the flour.

Preparation

1. Mix together the milk and 1½ tablespoons melted butter. If heating together, do not allow to boil.
2. Sift cassava flour and white flour together with salt and baking powder. Combine with milk and butter mixture. Add the Parmesan.
3. Beat well in the bowl of a stand mixer for about 3 minutes. Cover tightly with plastic wrap and let dough rest 30 minutes.
4. Preheat oven to 350°F.
5. Roll dough into balls about the size of Ping-Pong balls. Place on a greased and floured baking sheet, about ½ inch apart.
6. Bake approximately 20 minutes and cool on a wire rack.

Ingredients

- ½ cup warm milk
- 1½ tablespoons melted butter
- 1 cup cassava flour (some times called tapioca flour)
- ¾ cup white flour
- ½ teaspoon salt
- 1½ teaspoons baking powder
- ½ cup Parmesan

Difficulty

Easy

Preparation

1 and a half hours

Portion

12 to 15 rolls

ROSEMARY POPOVERS

I ate my first popovers in the cafeteria at Neiman Marcus in Chicago—and it was love at first taste! Look for a special popover pan, which has a deep, tapered shape and allows air to circulate around the popovers.

Preparation

2	eggs
½	teaspoon salt
1	cup milk
1	cup flour
	butter, softened, for greasing
1	teaspoon minced fresh rosemary

Ingredients

1. Preheat oven to 350°F. Grease eight popover molds with butter.
2. Beat eggs together with salt. Add milk and mix well.
3. In a separate bowl, sift the flour. Add the egg mixture until well blended.
4. Fill the popover molds three-quarters full, sprinkle the top of each popover with rosemary, and bake 40 to 50 minutes.
5. Remove popovers to a wire rack to cool, piercing the top of each with a knife to allow steam to escape. Serve warm.

Difficulty

Easy

Preparation

1 and a half hour

Portion

12 popovers

COLOMBIAN CHEESE BUNS

These traditional cheese buns—made with cornmeal and cassava flour—are called pan de bono (*or* pandebono) *in Colombia, where the bread originated.*

Ingredients

2	cups cornmeal
2	teaspoons baking powder
1	cup cassava flour (also called tapioca flour)
3	cups grated or crumbled semi-hard cheese, such as queso fresco or feta
16	ounces cream cheese
2	eggs, beaten

Preparation

1. Preheat oven to 350°F.
2. Mix all ingredients together in the bowl of a stand mixer.
3. Knead about 2 minutes, or until dough is smooth.
4. Form dough into balls about the size of walnuts, then roll the balls into log shapes, leaving a wider center. Curve into crescent shape.
5. Place 1 inch apart on a baking sheet lined with parchment paper.
6. Bake about 20 minutes, or just until rolls turn golden.

Difficulty

Easy

Preparation

1 hour

Portion

8 to 12 buns

BOLIVIAN CASSAVA BUNS

Called cuñapes, *these little cheese-flavored rolls are a popular snack and are also eaten for breakfast.*

Ingredients

- 2½ cups cassava flour (also called tapioca flour)
- ⅔ cup white flour
- 2 tablespoons baking powder
- ⅓ cup butter, softened
- 3 egg yolks
- 1 cup of milk, plus more as needed
- 2 cups finely grated or crumbled semi-hard cheese, like queso fresco or Cotija

Preparation

1. Preheat oven to 350°F.
2. Sift dry ingredients (cassava flour, white flour, and baking powder) together twice.
3. Mix butter into dry ingredients until a coarse meal forms. Make a mound with a well in the top.
4. Add the egg yolks and just enough milk to allow dough to form (begin with 1 cup and add slowly, stopping when flour is incorporated). Begin kneading by hand.
5. Once the ingredients are well combined, add in the cheese a little at a time. Add more milk if needed to keep dough smooth. It should be firm but not hard, and rather sticky.
6. Knead vigorously with the palms of your hands, until all the cheese is fully blended into the dough.
7. Form dough into balls about the size of a large walnut, and press your thumb into the bottoms to make a hollow. Place 1 inch apart on baking sheets that have been greased and floured or lined with parchment paper.
8. Bake until golden, 20 to 25 minutes. If you have a convection oven, do not use the fan. The bread must bake from the bottom up.

Difficulty

Easy

Preparation

1½ hours

Portion

15 to 20 buns

QUICK ROLLS WITH CHIVES AND CARAWAY

Butter makes these rolls nice and soft, and the combination of chives and caraway gives them a unique flavor.

Preparation

1. Preheat oven to 350°F.
2. Mix all ingredients in the bowl of a stand mixer with the dough hook attachment until a smooth dough forms, about 8 to 10 minutes.
3. Form small balls about the size of Ping-Pong balls and place them 1 inch apart on a baking sheet lined with parchment paper.
4. Bake until golden brown, about 30 minutes. Cool on a wire rack.

Ingredients

3 cups flour
1 tablespoon baking powder
1 teaspoon salt
½ cup finely chopped chives
1 tablespoon caraway seeds
½ cup (1 stick) butter, softened
1 cup evaporated milk
1 egg

Difficulty

Easy

Preparation

1 hour

Portion

30 to 36 rolls

DELIGHTFULLY SWEET QUICK BREADS

Anise-Flavored Bread • Banana Muffins • Carrot and Raisin Bread • Victorian Scones with Apricots • Zucchini–Raisin Bread

ANISE-FLAVORED BREAD

Halfway between cake and bread, this sweet bread flavored with anise is not to be missed. The recipe was a gift from my wonderful friend Betty!

Preparation

1. Preheat oven to 350°F.
2. Sift all dry ingredients together, except anise seeds.
3. Beat egg whites until stiff, about 3 minutes, and set aside.
4. Cream the butter with the shortening, add the 4 egg yolks and the beaten egg whites and mix well. Add flour mixture and anise seeds, combining well. Gradually add milk to the mixture, beating well, about 5 minutes.
5. Pour batter into a greased and floured 13-by-9-inch pan, and bake approximately 35 minutes.
6. Cool in pan on a wire rack.

Ingredients

4 cups flour
3 teaspoons baking powder
¼ teaspoon salt
1 cup sugar
4 egg yolks separated from whites
¼ cup (½ stick) butter
2 tablespoons shortening
1 tablespoon anise seeds
1 cup milk

Difficulty

Easy to Intermediate

Preparation

1 hour

Portion

24 to 30 servings

BANANA MUFFINS

This recipe is the easiest one in the book—and it's simply delicious.

Preparation

1. Preheat oven to 350°F.
2. Sift together flour, baking powder, baking soda, and salt. Set aside.
3. In a separate bowl, beat together egg, sugar, and butter. Mix in the mashed bananas and vanilla.
4. Add the dry ingredients to the wet ingredients, stirring until just combined. Finally, fold in the raisins.
5. Place paper baking cups in muffin tins and fill to two-thirds full.
6. Bake for approximately 18 to 20 minutes.
7. Let cool in tins for 5 minutes, then remove muffins to wire rack to cool completely. If desired, sift powdered sugar over muffins.

Ingredients

1½	cups flour
1	teaspoon baking powder
1	teaspoon baking soda
	pinch of salt
1	large egg
¾	cup sugar
⅓	cup melted butter
3	very ripe bananas, mashed
1	teaspoon vanilla
½	cup raisins, chopped
1	tablespoon powdered sugar, sifted (optional)

Difficulty

Easy

Preparation

45 minutes

Portion

12 muffins

CARROT AND RAISIN BREAD

Filled with healthy and delicious ingredients, this quick bread is incredibly easy to put together. Enjoy it with a good cup of strong coffee, or add it to your kids' lunchbox for a midday treat.

Ingredients

1½	cups flour
1	teaspoon baking powder
1	teaspoon baking soda
1	teaspoon salt
1	cup plus 2 tablespoons sugar
1	teaspoon ground cinnamon
1	cup vegetable oil
3	tablespoons molasses
3	eggs
1	teaspoon vanilla
1	cup shredded carrots
1	cup raisins
¾	cup chopped walnuts

Preparation

1. Grease and flour a loaf pan. Preheat oven to 350°F.
2. Combine flour, baking powder, baking soda, and salt.
3. In a separate bowl, mix sugar, cinnamon, oil, molasses, eggs, and vanilla, using hand mixer or stand mixer. Stir in the carrots by hand. Add the flour mixture to the mix of wet ingredients and combine well. Fold in raisins and walnuts.
4. Pour into the loaf pan and bake until golden brown, about 60 minutes.

Difficulty

Easy

Preparation

1½ hours

Portion

1 loaf

VICTORIAN SCONES WITH APRICOTS

A favorite for teatime, scones ideally have a thin, crisp exterior and fine, breadlike crumb inside. This version is baked as one large scone, then cut into slices for serving.

Preparation

1. Preheat oven to 400°F.
2. Grease and flour a 10-inch springform pan.
3. In a food processor, process flour, baking powder, sugar, salt, and butter to form a mixture that has the consistency of coarse meal.
4. Add eggs, cream, and vanilla, and process just until blended. Add apricots and nuts.
5. Spread dough in pan and bake until golden, 20 to 25 minutes. Release the springform, cut scone into wedges, and serve with Lemon Cream Cheese.
   Lemon Cream Cheese
1. Beat the cream cheese and sugar to a creamy consistency.
2. Stir in the lemon juice (adding more or less, depending on your taste), zest, and vanilla and mix until well combined.

Ingredients

2	cups flour
1	tablespoon baking powder
½	cup sugar
	pinch of salt
1	stick butter, cold, diced
2	eggs
⅓	cup heavy cream
1	tablespoon vanilla
½	cup finely chopped, dried apricots
½	cup walnuts, toasted and coarsely chopped

Lemon Cream Cheese

1	cup cream cheese
¼	cup powdered sugar
2–3	tablespoons lemon juice
½	teaspoon lemon zest
1	teaspoon vanilla

Difficulty

Intermediate

Preparation

1½ hours

Portion

12 scone wedges

ZUCCHINI–RAISIN BREAD

Gorgeous and easy, this moist quick bread gets its special flavor from a touch of orange.

Preparation

1. Preheat oven to 350°F.
2. Stir together the first nine ingredients, mixing well.
3. In a separate bowl, sift together flour, baking powder, and salt. Add the wet ingredients to the flour mixture, stirring until well combined. Fold in the walnuts.
4. Bake in a greased and floured loaf pan approximately 45 to 50 minutes. Cool on wire rack before removing loaf from pan.
5. To make glaze: stir sugar with vanilla and 2 tablespoons heavy cream, adding more cream as needed to attain the consistency of a thick liquid glaze. After the bread has cooled, drizzle with the glaze.

Ingredients

1½	cups sugar
2	teaspoons ground cinnamon
½	small orange, processed fine (peel and all)
1½	cups grated zucchini (with skin but without the seeds)
1	cup golden raisins
¼	cup (½ stick) butter, at room temperature
1	teaspoon vanilla
1⅓	cups warm water
1	egg, beaten
2⅓	cups flour
2	teaspoons baking powder pinch of salt
1	cup chopped toasted walnuts

For the glaze (optional):

1	cup powdered sugar, sifted
1	teaspoon vanilla
2–3	tablespoons heavy cream

Difficulty

Easy to Intermediate

Preparation

2 hours

Portion

1 loaf

HOLIDAY BREADS AND SPECIAL TREATS

Savory Stuffed Christmas Bread • Christmas Tree Bread with Chives
Jelly-Filled Doughnut Bites • Herbed Holiday Dinner Rolls • Cheese Sticks
Panettone • Poppy Seed Rolls • Christmas Candy Canes • Rugelach • Rum
Baba • Passover Bread • Deli-Style Rolls with Herbs for Passover • Pretzels
Sopaipillas

SAVORY STUFFED CHRISTMAS BREAD

This beautiful savory bread, which features traditional holiday red and green, is baked in a Christmas Tree–shaped pan.

Preparation

1. Make the filling: Cook the onion in butter on low heat until just turning translucent. Season to taste with salt and pepper.
2. Chop red bell peppers and strain.
3. Cook the spinach leaves in a little water. Remove and immerse immediately in ice water to stop cooking. Squeeze out water and chop spinach fine.
4. Stir together all filling ingredients and set aside.
5. Make the dough: Mix 4½ cups flour with yeast and stir well. Add salt and sugar and continue mixing well.
6. In a separate bowl, mix the 2 eggs, warm milk, and butter together. Add wet ingredients to the flour mixture. Add water slowly until all the loose flour is incorporated, using additional if necessary. The dough will be sticky.
7. Beat 5 minutes in a stand mixer fitted with dough hook.
8. Place in greased bowl and let rise 4 to 5 hours. Punch down dough, then knead in remaining ½ cup of flour.
9. Cut into two parts, one much larger than the other.
10. Grease and flour a pan shaped like a Christmas tree.
11. Press the larger piece of dough into the pan. Spread the filling over the dough.
12. On a lightly floured surface, stretch or roll out the smaller piece of dough. Cut circles of 2 to 2½ inches out of the dough. (These are the Christmas balls that will decorate the "tree.")
13. Place the circles over the filling so that they overlap one another. Use a small rectangular piece of dough to make a tree trunk and press to the bottom of the tree with a fork.
14. Brush the upper crust with egg yolk and sprinkle with sesame seeds.
15. Preheat oven to 400°F.
16. Let bread rise 30 minutes.
17. Bake until golden, about 45 to 60 minutes Serve warm.

Ingredients

For the filling:
- 2 onions, cut into strips
- salt and pepper, to taste
- 2 small red bell peppers
- 1 6–8 ounce bag spinach, leaves only
- 1½ cups ricotta cheese
- ½ cup cream cheese
- ½ cup Parmesan
- 1 cup chopped toasted walnuts
- 1 egg, beaten
- 1 ounce (¼ stick) butter

For the dough:
- 5 cups flour
- 1 tablespoon instant yeast
- 1 teaspoon salt
- ½ cup sugar
- 2 eggs
- ¾ cup warm milk
- ¼ cup melted butter
- ½ cup warm water, plus more as needed
- 1 egg yolk, beaten
- sesame seeds ,for sprinkling)

Difficulty

Intermediate

Preparation

5 hours

Portion

1 large bread

CHRISTMAS TREE BREAD WITH CHIVES

A special Christmas tree–shaped pan, see Savory Stuffed Christmas Bread for reference, together with the piquant flavor of chives, will make this bread the star of your holiday dinner.

Preparation

1. Grease and flour a pan shaped like a Christmas tree.
2. Melt butter and stir in the sour cream, 2 eggs, and chives.
3. Place 3 cups of the flour in the bowl of a stand mixer with the yeast, sugar, and salt. Mix well. Add the sour cream mixture and mix for a few more minutes. Add water slowly until there is no loose flour and a sticky dough has formed.
4. Cover and let rise at least 2 hours.
5. Preheat oven to 375°F.
   Roll dough into balls the size of a walnut. Brush balls with
6. beaten egg and milk mixture and roll them in seeds, alternating between poppy seeds and sesame seeds.
7. Place the dough balls in the pan close to each other, but leaving a small space, about ½ inch, between them. Let rise 15 minutes.
8. Bake until bread begins to brown, 35 to 45 minutes.

Ingredients

1 cup (2 sticks) butter
1 cup sour cream
2 eggs
⅔ cup finely chopped chives
6 cups flour
1 tablespoon instant yeast
⅔ cup sugar
1½ teaspoons salt
   warm water, as needed
1 egg, beaten with 2
   tablespoons milk
2 tablespoons poppy seeds
2 tablespoons sesame seeds

Difficulty

Easy

Preparation

4 to 5 hours

Portion

1 large bread

JELLY-FILLED DOUGHNUT BITES

These sweet little doughnut holes are filled with your favorite jam. You can make the dough a day in advance, refrigerate overnight, and then fry and fill with jam in the morning for a rich breakfast treat!

Ingredients

- 4 eggs
- 1 cup sugar
- ½ cup melted butter
- 1 ounce brandy or cognac
- 1 teaspoon vanilla
- 1½ cups warm milk
- ½ cup water
- 8 cups flour
- 2 tablespoons instant yeast
- 1 tablespoon salt
  vegetable oil, for frying
- 2 cups seedless jam,
    your favorite flavor
  sugar, for rolling the
    doughnut bites

Preparation

1. Beat eggs lightly and add the sugar.
2. In a separate bowl, mix butter, cognac, and vanilla with milk and water. Add to egg mixture.
3. Add flour, yeast, and salt to the wet ingredients until just incorporated. The dough will be very sticky.
4. Stir and let the dough rise for 2 to 3 hours, or until it doubles in size.
5. Knead for a few minutes.
6. Roll out dough to a thickness of about ⅓ inch. Cut seventy-two 2- to 2½-inch circles.
7. Let rest 10 to 15 minutes and then fry in hot oil at 350°F until golden, about 5 to 8 minutes.
8. Let doughnut holes drain on paper towels and cool a bit, then fill with jam. You can use a pastry bag and insert the tip into the doughnut bite to fill. Roll in sugar to finish.

Difficulty

Intermeate

Preparation

5 hours

Portion

72 donut bites

142

HERBED HOLIDAY DINNER ROLLS

At Christmastime, I like to bake these herb-flavored rolls in my Christmas tree–shaped pan for a stunning presentation on the holiday table!

Preparation

1. Combine ½ cup milk with herbs, butter, sugar, and salt. Heat in a pan until butter melts. Let cool and mix with eggs.
2. In a separate bowl, mix together the flour, powdered milk, and yeast, then combine with egg and milk mixture. Add more milk if necessary until dough is sticky. Beat until dough is smooth, about 5 minutes.
3. Let rise 2 to 3 hours.
4. Form balls the size of a walnut and place them about ½ inch apart on a greased and floured baking sheet. Let rise 30 minutes.
5. While rolls are rising, preheat oven to 400°F.
6. Brush the rolls with melted butter and bake for 15 to 20 minutes. Cool on wire rack.

Ingredients

½   cup whole milk, plus more as needed
2   tablespoons chopped fresh basil
1   tablespoon chopped fresh rosemary
1   tablespoon finely chopped fresh oregano
1   tablespoon chopped fresh sage
½   cup (1 stick) butter
⅓   cup sugar
2   teaspoons salt
3   eggs
4   cups flour
3   tablespoons powdered milk
1½ tablespoons instant yeast
    melted butter, for brushing

Difficulty

Easy to intermediate

Preparation

4 hours

Portion

12 to 18 rolls

CHEESE STICKS

These cheese sticks are oh-so-easy to make! A dash of cayenne spices them up a bit and brings out the flavor of the cheddar.

  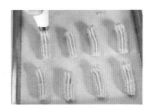

Preparation

1. Preheat oven to 350°F.
2. Stir together all ingredients except flour. Once all ingredients are mixed, incorporate the flour until well combined.
3. Put the dough into a pastry bag fitted with a star tip. Line baking sheets with parchment paper. Pipe the dough onto the baking sheets in sticks of about 3 to 4 inches in length.
4. Bake about until golden, about 15 minutes.

Ingredients

1	cup butter (2 sticks), softened
1	egg yolk
1	egg
½	teaspoon cayenne pepper
1	teaspoon salt
3	tablespoons cream cheese
1 ½	cups shredded cheddar cheese
⅓–½	cup grated Parmesan
2	tablespoons milk plus, extra if needed
1½	cups flour

Difficulty
Easy

Preparation
1½ hours

Portion
24 to 30 sticks

PANETTONE

Studded with candied fruit and raisins and dusted with powdered sugar, this glorious confection is a showstopper. Is this delicious treat a bread or a cake? While I do not know the answer, I do know this panettone is spectacular!

Preparation

1. In a bowl, mix together 1 cup of flour, the yeast, and the water. Stir well. Let this mixture fluff for about 1 hour.
2. Stir together the remaining flour, the sugar, and the salt, and add to the dough starter. Add the yogurt, butter, vanilla, and the eggs and egg yolks, and beat well in a heavy stand mixer.
3. Add the fruits, zest, nuts, and seeds and mix well.
4. Place dough in a greased bowl, cover it, and let it rise at least 3 or 4 hours, until it is doubled in size.
5. Knead 5 or 6 minutes, and form a ball.
6. Place the dough in a panettone pan that has been greased and floured. Alternatively, use paper panettone molds, which can be found in specialty baking stores and online.
7. Preheat oven to 375°F.
8. Let dough rise another 30 minutes.
9. Cut a cross on top of the bread. Brush with beaten egg and cover the top with foil.
10. Bake for about 15 minutes, then remove the foil. Continue baking until panettone is browned, about another 15 minutes (total baking time is approximately 30 minutes), or until toothpick inserted comes out clean.
11. As soon as the panettone comes out of the oven, sprinkling with powdered sugar.

Ingredients

4½	cups flour, plus extra
2	tablespoons instant yeast
½	cup warm water
⅔	cup sugar
1	teaspoon salt
½	cup plain yogurt or buttermilk
6	ounces melted butter
1	tablespoon vanilla
4	whole eggs plus 2 yolks
¾	cup finely chopped candied fruit
½	cup chopped maraschino cherries
¾	cup raisins cut with scissors
	zest of 1 lemon
	zest of 1 orange
½	cup blanched almonds or pine nuts, toasted
⅛	teaspoon crushed anise seeds
1	egg, beaten
	powdered sugar (for sprinkling)

Difficulty

Intermediate

Preparation

4 hours

Portion

1 loaf

POPPY SEED ROLLS

This old-world favorite features tender dough wrapped around a sweet poppy seed filling. Delicious!

Ingredients

- 3 cups flour, plus extra
- 2 teaspoons baking powder
- pinch of salt
- ¾ cup sugar
- 4 tablespoons lukewarm milk
- 4 tablespoons sour cream
- 1 cup (2 sticks) butter, cold
- 1 egg, beaten
- 2 egg yolks

For the filling:
- 1½ cups poppy seeds
- ¾ cup sugar
- 2 tablespoons honey
- ½ cup milk
- zest of 1 orange
- 1 tablespoon pure cocoa powder
- ½ cup raisins

Preparation

1. Mix flour, baking powder, and salt. Add sugar.
2. In a separate bowl combine milk, 1 beaten egg, 2 egg yolks, and sour cream.
3. Using a pastry blender or two butter knives, cut the butter into the flour to make a fine meal. Add the milk and egg mixture, and mix until the dough forms a ball.
4. Roll the dough into a rectangle 24 by 36 inches and fold into three, as if you were folding a letter into an envelope. Refrigerate 20 minutes. Roll out again and make the same folds. Refrigerate overnight, or at least 8 hours.
5. Make the filling: Stir all filling ingredients together in a saucepan and bring to a boil. Cool before using.
6. Preheat oven to 375°F.
7. Roll out dough again, and divide into four pieces.
8. Roll each piece into a rectangle about 4½ by 6 inches. Spread each with a quarter of the filling and roll tightly.
9. Brush the top with remaining beaten egg and bake until golden, 25 to 30 minutes.

Difficulty

Intermediate

Preparation

4 hours plus overnight

Portion

4 large rolls

CHRISTMAS CANDY CANES

These festive breads—filled with dried and candied fruits, then shaped into candy canes— will wow your guests. They also make special gifts!

Preparation

1. Make the dough: Add honey to warm water and stir. Dissolve yeast in water and let sit 10 minutes, tightly covered.
2. Combine the flour, salt, sugar, sour cream, butter, and eggs in stand mixer and add water until dough is firm but sticky. Beat 8 minutes.
3. Place dough in oiled plastic bag and let double in size, about 2 to 3 hours.
4. Make the filling: mix together all filling ingredients and set aside.
5. Preheat oven to 375°F.
6. Punch down dough and divide in two. Roll into two rectangles, about 12 by 20 inches. Place the filling down the center of each rectangle, then cut each side of the rectangle in diagonal strips about 1 inch wide, similar to thick fringe. Close the loaf by folding alternating strips in a crisscross pattern toward the center of the dough.
7. Form the long bread into a candy cane shape. Brush with beaten egg yolk and milk, and let stand 20 minutes.
8. Bake until golden, approximately 35 minutes.
9. While canes are baking, make glaze: add water to powdered sugar, stirring until a thin icing forms. Drizzle with glaze once canes have cooled slightly.

Ingredients

For the dough:
1 tablespoon honey
½ cup warm water
2 tablespoons granulated dry yeast
7 cups flour
2 teaspoons salt
⅔ cup sugar
2 cups sour cream
¼ cup (½ stick) butter, softened
2 eggs
warm water, as needed
1 egg yolk beaten with 1 teaspoon milk
For the filling:
1 cup green candied cherries
1 cup red candied cherries
½ cup chopped raisins
1 cup chopped apricots
1 cup chopped toasted walnuts
⅓ cup sugar
¼ cup (½ stick) butter
3 slices sandwich bread, crusts removed, broken into crumbs
For the glaze:
2 cups powdered sugar, sifted
2–3 tablespoons boiling water

Difficulty

Easy to intermediate

Preparation

4 to 5 hours

Portion

2 loaves

RUGELACH

These treats are a bit of work, but they are worth the effort! You can make them in advance, and then on the day you are serving them, simply place the rugelach in a preheated 350ºF oven for just a few minutes to crisp them up.

Preparation

1. Make the filling: Mix together sugar and cinnamon. Combine the cinnamon–sugar mixture with the ¼ cup walnuts. If you are using the preserves option instead, combine the preserves with 2 tablespoons walnuts.
2. Make the dough: Cream together butter and cream cheese. Incorporate flour until you have a sticky yet manageable dough. Do not knead, just combine well. Refrigerate 24 hours.
3. Preheat oven to 350ºF.
4. Cut dough into three pieces. With a rolling pin, roll one piece of dough into a circle, to a thickness of about 1/8 inch. Cut the circle into six to eight small triangles, as you would a pizza. Alternatively, use a cookie cutter to cut the triangles. Repeat with the other two pieces of dough.
5. Spread filling at each triangle's base and roll from the base of the triangle to the tip.
6. Combine the ¼ cup sugar, 1 tablespoon cinnamon, and 1 tablespoon chopped walnuts and sprinkle over rugelach
7. Bake until rugelach begin to brown, about 20 to 25 minutes.
8. Cool on a wire rack.

Ingredients

For the filling:
- ½ cup sugar
- 1 tablespoon ground cinnamon
- ¼ cup finely chopped walnuts

Alternative filling:
- ½ cup orange marmalade or pineapple preserves (or jam of your choice)
- 2 tablespoons finely chopped walnuts

For the dough:
- 1 cup (2 sticks) butter, softened
- 6 ounces cream cheese
- 2¼ cups flour

For sprinkling:
- ¼ cup sugar
- 1 tablespoon ground cinnamon
- 1 tablespoon finely chopped walknuts

Difficulty

Intermediate

Preparation

3 hours and 1 day

Portion

18 to 24 rugelach

RUM BABA

These little yeast-risen cakes, soaked in spiced rum, are made with a dough even richer than that for brioche. They are best baked in special baba molds—but you can use a cupcake pan if you don't have the molds. Some bakers use an angel food cake pan to make a large baba.

Preparation

1. Make the syrup: Mix all ingredients, except the rum, in a heavy saucepan and simmer 2 minutes. Turn off the heat and add the rum. Let cool and strain.
2. Make the dough: By hand, mix the flour with the salt and sugar. Add yeast, milk, and eggs, and mix well. Allow the dough to rest for 30 minutes. Integrate the butter and beat a few more minutes.
3. Cover and let the dough double in size, about 2 hours. Put the dough in a piping bag and fill greased and floured baba molds. Let dough stand 20 minutes.
4. Preheat oven to 325°F.
5. Bake until golden, 20 to 25 minutes.
6. Pour the syrup over the warm baba and place on a wire rack to drain.
7. Using a star tip fitted to your pastry bag, fill the center of each baba with whipped cream. Decorate with fruits.

Ingredients

For the syrup:
1⅓ cups sugar
2 cups water
2 cinnamon sticks
    peel of 1 orange
    peel of 1 lemon
2 cloves
1 star anise
⅓–½ cup rum
For the dough:
2½ cups flour
½ teaspoon salt
1 ½ tablespoons sugar
1 teaspoon instant yeast
¾ cups milk
4 eggs
½ cup (1 stick) butter, softened
For the fillling and garnish:
1½ cups whipped cream
3 cups total (approximately) various fruits, such as kiwi, strawberries, orange slices
    mint leaves

Difficulty

Intermediate

Preparation

4 to 5 hours

Portion

8 baba

PASSOVER BREAD

These versatile unleavened rolls can be served for breakfast or for other meals throughout Passover.

Ingredients

2	cups matzo meal
1	teaspoon salt
1	tablespoon sugar
1	cup water
½	cup vegetable oil
4	large eggs
	extra oil, for hands

Preparation

1. Preheat oven to 375°F. Grease a baking sheet.
2. Mix the matzo meal, salt, and sugar in a mixer.
3. In a saucepan, bring the water and the oil to a boil; slowly add to the matzo mixture. Mix well.
4. Add the eggs one by one and beat a few minutes. Let dough rest at least 30 minutes.
5. Oil your hands and form balls the size of golf balls. Make a hole in the center to form a bagel shape. Place 1 inch apart on greased baking sheet. (Oil your hands again whenever the dough begins to stick to them.)
6. Cover with aluminum foil and bake 25 minutes. Remove aluminum foil and bake about another 20 minutes.
7. Serve warm.

Difficulty

Easy

Preparation

2 hours

Portion

12 to 16 rolls

DELI-STYLE ROLLS WITH HERBS FOR PASSOVER

Featuring Italian herbs for added zest, these rolls are made rich with eggs.

Preparation

1. Preheat oven to 350°F.
2. Bring water, butter, and salt to a boil.
3. Add the matzo meal and herbs all at once and cook, stirring, about 2 minutes. Place mixture in the bowl of a mixer.
4. Add eggs one at a time, beating at high speed. Place dough by tablespoonfuls on baking sheets lined with parchment paper and bake until golden, about 30 minutes. Do not open the oven while the dough is raw—the cooler air will interfere with the baking process.

Ingredients

1 cup water
½ cup (1 stick) butter
1 teaspoon salt
1½ cups matzo meal
1 tablespoon Italian herbs
5 eggs

Difficulty

Easy

Preparation

1 hour

Portion

12 to 16 rolls

PRETZELS

Homemade pretzels are a fun project to do with the kids. They'll have a great time rolling and forming the classic pretzel shapes—and they'll enjoy eating them even more!

Preparation

1. Combine the warm water with the yeast in the bowl of a stand mixer and let sit 5 to 7 minutes. Gradually add 1⅓ cups water, brown sugar, salt, baking soda, onion, and flour. If desired, add one tablespoon of Dijon mustard to the dough. Beat until a ball of dough forms, and continue beating until dough is smooth (add a little more flour if needed to make a smooth dough).
2. Cut dough into pieces the size of a golf ball. Cover and rest 10 minutes.
3. Stretch the dough and form long ropes. Form a pretzel shape, rolling and pressing the ends toward the center.
4. Bring a large pot of water to a boil. Meanwhile, line baking sheets with parchment paper.
5. Preheat oven to 375°F.
6. Drop the pretzels one by one into the boiling water for 20 seconds on each side. When they come out of the water, place on baking sheet lined with parchment paper.
7. Brush with egg white and sprinkle with coarse salt. Bake until golden, 18 to 25 minutes.
8. Optional: During last 10 minutes of baking, sprinkle pretzels with chopped basil and minced garlic or grated cheddar .

Ingredients

4	tablespoons warm water
2	tablespoons active dry yeast
1⅓	cups warm water
⅓	cup brown sugar
1½	teaspoons salt
½	cup baking soda
1	onion, grated
5	cups flour, plus extra if needed
1	teaspoon Dijon mustard (optional)
1	egg white, beaten coarse salt (for sprinkling)
2	tablespoons chopped basil and garlic (optional)
1	cup grated cheddar (optional)

Difficulty

Advanced

Preparation

3 to 4 hours

Portion

36 to 48 pretzels

SOPAIPILLAS

This fried bread is a favorite in South America, and its appeal has spread throughout the American Southwest, though recipes and traditions vary from place to place. The Chilean version of sopaipillas represented here is served with **pebre,** *a condiment made primarily of cilantro, onions, and garlic... delicious! Thanks to my friend Alonso for the recipe.*

Preparation

1. Sift flour with salt and baking powder.
2. Beat the shortening and warm water, adding as much as is necessary to form a dough that does not stick to your hands.
3. Cover dough with plastic and let stand about 30 minutes. Roll or stretch the dough to a thickness of about ½ inch.
4. Cut into 2½-inch circles and fry in hot oil.
5. Serve with Cilantro Salsa.
   Cilantro Salsa
   Stir together the cilantro, onion, garlic, lemon juice, white vinegar, water, salt, pepper, and oil.

Ingredients

3	cups flour
½	teaspoon salt
2	teaspoons baking powder
2	tablespoon shortening
1	cup warm water, approximately
	oil, for frying
	Cilantro Salsa
⅔	cup finely chopped cilantro
1	onion, chopped fine
2	cloves garlic, minced fine
¼	cup lemon juice
¼	cup white wine vinegar
¼	cup water
	salt and pepper, to taste
2	tablespoons vegetable oil

Difficulty

Intermediate

Preparation

1½ hours

Portion

12 to 18 loaves

ABOUT THE AUTHOR

Doris Kohn Gudes, better known as Doris Goldgewicht, was born in Costa Rica and has lived there most of her life. She has been passionate about cooking and baking since she was a small child. She began her culinary studies at the National Training Institute (INA) in Costa Rica, and has studied abroad, in the United States at the Cochran Program of the United States Embassy, as well as in Vermont and New Orleans. She has also studied in South America, at programs in Argentina and Bolivia. Goldgewicht graduated as Chef Instructor–Advisor, certified by the World Association of Cook's Societies (WACS) and the National Association of Chefs of Costa Rica (ANCH), where for two years she held a seat on the board.

Before embarking on her culinary training, Goldgewicht pursued a degree in psychology, graduating with honors from the University of Costa Rica. Along with four colleagues, she founded a mental health clinic in San José, Costa Rica. But she could not forget her passion for cooking, so she set aside her work in psychology and began her career as a culinary instructor. She teaches and participates as a partner in top national newspapers and magazines in Costa Rica.

For six years, Goldgewicht starred in her own television show, *Doris Without Secrets*, publishing bimonthly cookbooks that featured recipes from the program. A lover of Costa Rican cuisine, Goldgewicht next created, with her friend chef Carlos Rodriguez, a television series called *Taste and Sazon*, which tours Costa Rica in search of distinctive local cuisine. This show is a favorite of food lovers everywhere—and thanks to the Internet, it is seen across the world, with many viewers in the United States, Canada, and across Central America.

As one of her many projects, Goldgewicht manages food handling through Serv Safe New York and helps establish Costa Rican food safety standards. Her love for Costa Rica led to publication of a bilingual book called Secrets of Costa Rican Cuisine, which explores the rich history of Costa Rica's food traditions. She loves baking, and has produced booklets on both cakes and chocolate. Today, Goldgewicht is a member of ULADES (Latin Union of High Schools), an organization whose purpose is to educate youth about regional cuisine and their Latin American heritage.

Now, Goldgewicht can again be seen on Costa Rican national television, in a program called Sabores, a multimedia presentation that you can also streams on the internet Monday to Friday. She continues to enjoy teaching as well.

APPENDIX

Making Dulce de Leche

Some of the recipes in *Home-Baked Breads* call for dulce de leche. Depending on your local supermarket, you may find it jarred on store shelves. But if you can't—or if you prefer homemade—this confection is easy to make at home. There are many, many recipes—a simple internet search for "dulce de leche recipes" will turn up tens of thousands. Here is one simple method that doesn't require constant watching on a stove:

Homemade Dulce de Leche

1 can sweetened condensed milk

Preheat oven to 425° F.

Pour the can of sweetened condensed milk into a shallow baking dish. Set the baking dish into a larger pan. Add hot water to the larger pan until it reaches halfway up the side of the baking dish. Cover the baking dish tightly with aluminum foil and bake for 1 hour. Check the pan periodically, adding more water to the outer pan as necessary. Once the condensed milk is nicely browned, remove the dish from the oven and let cool. When the mixture has cooled, whisk it until it is smooth. Store the dulce de leche in sterilized glass jars in the refrigerator until ready to use.

Yeast Equivalents

1 teaspoon instant yeast = 1½ teaspoons active dry yeast = 2 teaspoons fresh yeast (packed)

General Measuring Equivalents

1 pinch = less than ½ teaspoon (dry)
1 dash = 3 drops to ¼ teaspoon (liquid)
1½ teaspoons = ½ tablespoons = ¼ ounce
3 teaspoons = 1 tablespoon = ½ ounce
2 tablespoons = 1 ounce
4 tablespoons = 2 ounces = ¼ cup
8 tablespoons = 4 ounces = ½ cups
16 tablespoons = 8 ounces = 1 cup = ½ pound
32 tablespoons = 16 ounces = 2 cups = 1 pound
4 cups = 1 quart

Metric Conversions
(Conversions are approximate)

Measurements

Imperial	Metric
¼ teaspoon	1 ml
½ teaspoon	2 ml
1 teaspoon	5 ml
1 tablespoon	15 ml
2 tablespoons	25 ml
3 tablespoons	50 ml
¼ cup	50 ml
⅓ cup	75 ml
½ cup	125 ml
⅔ cup	150 ml
3/4 cup	175 ml
1 cup	250 ml

Temperature

Fahrenhiet	Celsius
32°	0°
212°	100°
250°	121°
275°	140°
300°	150°
325°	160°
350°	180°
375°	190°
400°	200°
425°	220°
450°	230°
475°	240°

Yields for Common Baking Ingredients
(Yields are approximate)

Ingredient	The recipe calls for:	You will need:
Butter	1 cup	2 sticks
Chocolate chips	1 cup	6 ounces
Cheese, grated	1 cup	4 ounces
Cream Cheese	1 cup	8 ounces
Dates	2½ cups, pitted	1 pound
Flour, all-purpose	3½ cups	1 pound
Honey	1 cup	12 ounces
Raisins	1 cup	5 ounces
Semolina	1 cup	6 ounces
Sugar, granulated	2 cup	1 pound
Sugar, powdered	4 cup	1 pound
Walnuts	4 cup	1 pound

Baking Resources

Following is a selected list of online suppliers that carry baking and kitchen equipment and/or flours. A quick search will yield hundreds of others, likely including some specialty baking shops in your area.

Bob's Red Mill
Flours and grains, including some hard-to-find products.
www.bobsredmill.com

Breadtopia
A full range of equipment for bread baking.
www.breadtopia.com

Broadway Panhandler
Bakeware and kitchen equipment, including Pullman bread pans.
www.broadwaypanhandler.com

Chicago Metallic
Bakeware and specialty pans.
www.chicagometallicbakeware.com

Hodgson Mill
Flours, including many stone-ground flours.
www.hodgsonmill.com

JB Prince
Equipment and pans, including sous vide supplies.
www.jbprince.com

King Arthur Flour
High-quality bread flours and specialty flours.
www.kingarthurflour.com

Wilton
Baking equipment, including shaped cake pans and pastry bags and tips.
www.wilton.com

INDEX